An Examination
of
The Shelley Legend

An Examination
of
The Shelley Legend

By

NEWMAN I. WHITE · FREDERICK L. JONES

KENNETH N. CAMERON

Philadelphia

UNIVERSITY OF PENNSYLVANIA PRESS

1951

Copyright 1951

UNIVERSITY OF PENNSYLVANIA PRESS

Manufactured in the United States of America

LONDON: GEOFFREY CUMBERLEGE
OXFORD UNIVERSITY PRESS

*The publication of this volume has been
aided by a grant from the
Carl and Lily Pforzheimer Foundation, Inc.*

Contents

Introduction

When *The Shelley Legend*[1] was published in 1945, it was immediately hailed by the reviewers for our most popular and highly respected periodicals as a very important book. One went so far as to say that "Perhaps more than anyone who has written of Shelley in the 123 years since his death, Dr. Smith has shown us the whole melodramatic set of circumstances as they were." Another classed the book as "quite obviously an indispensable piece of research"; a third was of the opinion that "there can be no doubt that he [the author] has opened the windows of a very fetid room and let in a blast of fresh air," for which, he thinks, "we may be grateful"; a fourth called it "an aggressive, controversial, inevitable, and necessary book." All these, and others, accepted with scarcely a hint of doubt the main thesis of the book: that the real Shelley is still unknown to us because the documentary foundation of Shelley scholarship is unsound, many documents having been withheld, destroyed, expurgated, or forged.

The literary public was astonished and disgusted with this state of affairs, which promised to lead to a situation as shocking to literary scholarship as the famous T. J. Wise forgeries of nineteenth century pamphlets. A few unwary scholars began making loose and hasty conjectures about the authenticity of important manuscripts which hitherto there had been no reason to suspect.

[1] *The Shelley Legend*, by Robert M. Smith in collaboration with Martha M. Schlegel, Theodore G. Ehrsam, and Louis A. Waters. New York: Charles Scribner's Sons, 1945. vii + 343 pp.

Though obviously chaotic in arrangement and sensational in purpose—facts not unnoticed by the reviewers—*The Shelley Legend* was taken seriously and was proving dangerous. It was therefore necessary for some who were more thoroughly acquainted with Shelley scholarship, especially the biographical and manuscript phases of it, to demonstrate that *The Shelley Legend* was the most incompetent book ever written on Shelley and that none of its startling claims about forgeries and a family-created legend were true. This exposure was accomplished mainly by the three articles printed in this volume. Each attacks *The Shelley Legend* from a different point of view and therefore conjointly they illuminate the subject as no article alone does. Professor Newman I. White reveals the ignorance of the authors, their innumerable errors, and the falsity of their charges against his own biography of Shelley. My article shows, I trust, that the documentary foundation of Shelley scholarship is perfectly sound, and that all the furor about forgeries is nothing more than a bogy created by the authors themselves. Professor Kenneth N. Cameron's article demonstrates that the real Shelley whom the authors claim to have revealed is a ghastly caricature.

Under this triple attack *The Shelley Legend* died in less than a year after its publication. Nor is there any danger that it will ever be resurrected as a trustworthy book. It is still sitting on library shelves, however, and is occasionally confusing students who approach Shelley for the first time. Since it is not likely that beginners will dig up these articles from the scholarly journals in which they were originally published, it seems fitting that they should be available to them in the same library catalogues and on the library shelves where they meet with *The Shelley Legend*. And that is the principal aim of this volume.

It will be of interest to note that Mr. Theodore G. Ehrsam,

who wrote virtually everything in *The Shelley Legend* with reference to forgeries, took the trouble in the summer of 1949 to examine in the British Museum the Wise manuscript of Shelley's letter of December 16, 1816, to Mary, which forms the chief exhibit of forgeries in *The Shelley Legend*. In the London *Times Literary Supplement* for September 30, 1949 (p. 633) he declares this letter in every way genuine, except for the signature. Mr. Ehrsam made no reference to *The Shelley Legend*, but was sharply reminded of it in the *Supplement* for October 7 (p. 649) by Miss Sylva Norman, who was mystified by his recantation. Mr. Ehrsam replied in the November 4 issue (p. 715), giving a history of his further researches and the reasons for his "complete change of front" (as Miss Norman had called it). The series of letters in the *Supplement* concluded on November 11 (p. 733), with Miss Norman's applause for Mr. Ehrsam's "courage and honesty" and a brief account, "for the benefit of English readers," of *The Shelley Legend;* she refers to it as "this misguided publication of 1945" and to its "inglorious collapse."

Quite independently Mr. Andreas Mayor, of England, examined the Wise manuscript of Shelley's letter of December 16, 1816, in the British Museum. He also pronounced it genuine except for the signature, and published his findings as "A Suspected Shelley Letter," in *The Library:* Transactions of the Bibliographical Society, Fifth Series, IV (September, 1949), 141-145.

The finishing blow has been struck by Mr. Ehrsam himself. In April 1951 he published *Major Byron, The Incredible Career of a Literary Forger* (New York: Charles S. Boesen). This book not only authenticates the Wise copy of the famous letter of December 16, 1816, to Mary, but also declares as genuine originals every single item which had been labeled as a forgery by *The Shelley Legend*. Mr. Ehrsam rather naïvely traces his former errors and those of his colleagues in this way: "But was there some small circumstance which had actually given rise to this devious trail of suspicion? Yes; it was merely a forged signature, precisely and accurately tacked on to a genuine Shelley letter [that of December 16, 1816] long years after Shelley's death . . . doubt cast on this single letter by this one forged signature spread wide to include other letters equally genuine" (p. 189).

It should be added that the three articles are reproduced in this volume exactly as they were originally published, except for the first footnote in each (these being the same kind of bibliographical note) and the correction of a few typographical errors.

FREDERICK L. JONES

Philadelphia, Pa.

An Examination

of

The Shelley Legend

The Shelley Legend Examined[1]

Newman I. White

THE PUBLISHERS claim for this book that it dispels the "mirages and myths that have obscured the real Shelley," and reviewers have been inclined to accept this claim without analyzing it. This paper provides an analysis. Since it is impossible to refer with certainty every individual statement to its particular author, I shall refer them all to Professor Smith, who is clearly the directing genius.

Professor Smith tells us in his Preface that the "Shelley Legend" is a term representing the "fallacious views about the life of Shelley and his writings" which started with Mary Shelley, and spread and ramified under the patronage of Lady Shelley and her husband, the poet's son. Its influence, he asserts later, practically vitiated even the twentieth-century biographies of the poet. The purpose of the book is to "expose what we believe to be the fraudulent and mistaken efforts" by which these practices changed Shelley into something quite contrary to the real Shelley. The methods employed are the examination of suspected documents by handwriting experts, the searching of correspondence, diaries, memoirs, sales records, etc., and the combination of the results into a picture of the "legend" by means of deduction and inference.

It was Mary Shelley, according to Professor Smith, who

---

[1] Originally published in *Studies in Philology* (XLIII, July 1946, 522-544), and reprinted here by permission of Mrs. Newman I. White and the Editor of *Studies in Philology*.

created the "Shelley Legend," by editing Shelley's published works, seeking to influence or control what others (e.g., Trelawny and Medwin) wrote about him, encouraging Hogg and Leigh Hunt to write about him, marrying her son to a rich wife likely to continue the tradition, giving silent or roundabout support to misrepresentations of Shelley's first wife, Harriet, collecting Shelley's letters, glossing over or playing down unfavorable facts in her writing, and removing from her journal passages that were presumably unfavorable.

None of this is really new or remarkable. I have pointed out myself, more than once, the various ways in which Mary Shelley sought to promote and enhance her husband's reputation. There is scarcely a detail among those listed above that cannot be gleaned directly from my two-volume *Shelley*. In the same position, probably nine widows out of ten would have done precisely as Mary did.

Yet probably many of Professor Smith's readers will see these actions in a different light as they read his account. The difference is due to the fact that Professor Smith has closely linked his case with an attack on Mary's character. Impatient, usually unspecific utterances of Trelawny, Byron, and Lady Blessington are quoted (sometimes more than once) to damn her; her life with Shelley is reviewed unfavorably, with some factual distortion, and always in language colored by the author's point of view without logical justification. In the biographies, diaries, letters, and works of Mary Shelley I have found far more testimonials for than against her. Professor Smith has ignored all these. His exclusion of favorable testimony and his coloring of factual statements by his own preconceived opinions suggest more the vigorous prosecuting attorney with an eye on the next election than the responsible scholar attempting to fix the truth.

One may well wonder how Mary's character enters into the purely factual record of what she did or didn't do to es-

tablish the "Shelley Legend." Her character gains more significance, however, in connection with the "forged" Shelley
documents to which Professor Smith devotes so much attention. It has been known for some time that in 1845 the forger,
later known as "Major Byron," approached Mary, through
her friend, Thomas Hookham, and endeavored to sell letters
which he claimed had been acquired through a former landlord of the Shelleys at Marlow. Mary Shelley's letters in this
affair show clearly that she regarded the man with distaste
and suspicion, but felt that she must recover the letters, some
of which she bought. There is no evidence as to whether or
not some of her purchases were genuine or whether or not
Mary believed any of them to be forgeries. In either case her
motive for purchasing would be presumed to be the obvious,
straightforward one, lacking definite evidence to the contrary.
To Professor Smith, however, convinced from the start that
Mary is unscrupulous, these transactions seem highly suspicious. They are the chief basis of repeated suggestions of
Mary's guilty connivance with a forger—and they have no
more solid foundation than Professor Smith's unfavorable
general view of her character.

It hardly seems likely that Mary Shelley could have been
acting in guilty connivance with a forger and at the same time
filling her letters to Hookham with her constant suspicion
that this collaborator was a thief and a crook. But Professor
Smith finds it highly significant that four of the letters which
he believes to be Major Byron forgeries happen to attack
Harriet Shelley's character. These attacks on Harriet's character he considers were also one of the main objects of Mary
and Lady Shelley; and since he charges that Lady Shelley consciously used these forgeries for that purpose, he is convinced,
and repeatedly suggests, without charging outright, that the
family employed the forger. This scandalous and irresponsible
suggestion is made without producing any evidence of com-

munication or contact between Lady Shelley and the forger, and it would be merely a wild suspicion if the letters attacking Harriet were really forgeries. But when we see—as I shall show later—that the contents of these letters are almost certainly genuine, the whole point becomes absurd.

This question of character later becomes an indirect argument both in the treatment of Mary's affair with Hogg and in the Hoppner Scandal—but long before then Professor Smith has become the victim of circular argument. In the last analysis Mary (and also Lady Shelley) are supposed to be guilty of particular, reprehensible acts because they are reprehensible persons, and the same reprehensible acts (thus established) are further proof that they are reprehensible persons.

*   *   *   *   *

The "Legend" continues with Lady Shelley, who inherited it from her mother-in-law, Mary Shelley. For a generation or two, at least, there has always been a pretty general agreement about Lady Shelley among Shelley scholars. She has been regarded as officious and overbearing, a bossy woman with an inaccurate mind, who felt that Shelley belonged first to the family and next to the world, and who may have felt that the control of manuscripts carried with it the control of the facts they contained and the scholars who used them. Half the biographers who ever wrote have probably had some similar person to contend with.

On this point Professor Smith was anticipated over sixty years ago, when Mr. J. Cordy Jeaffreson, a lawyer rather than a professional scholar, produced his *The Real Shelley* (1885). This book is a rude, but acute outcry against Lady Shelley's attempted dominance and the la-de-da-ism in Shelleyan circles that may have been partly due to it and partly to the manners of the time. It performed the real service, though perhaps too crudely, of putting Shelley scholars forever on their guard against undue family influence. *The Real Shelley* is the direct ancestor of *The Shelley Legend,* which is only a dose of the same medicine, with more violent ingredients added. These additions consist mainly in the charges that Lady Shelley abetted slander against Harriet by the use of forged documents which she knew to have been forged. It is not even considered (1) that the charges against Harriet may have been true, or (2) that Lady Shelley may have believed them to be true. Since neither proposition can be proved either true or false, it is begging the question to assume both of them false. Lady Shelley was under no obligation to believe in Harriet's innocence, and her strong affection for Mary could easily have convinced such a person of Harriet's guilt.

With all of his aspersions on her character, Professor Smith has produced no tangible evidence to show that Lady Shelley was either a deliberate liar or a person who would deal with or countenance forgery. His "evidence" in the present case is largely his own suspicion, and it breaks down on a number of points. In the first place, if she were consciously using forgeries, would she have raised the question of forgery herself? Yet it was she who first clearly denounced the letter of December 15-16, 1816 (the most important of the lot), as a forged copy (p. 92). In the second place, the most important of these "forged" letters, and probably of the others, is almost certainly a copy of a genuine original, if not genuine itself; and in the third place there is clear evidence that the charges in the "forged" letters were made elsewhere and that Lady Shelley therefore was not compelled to depend upon forgeries. These points will all be elaborated later, in a discussion of the forgeries themselves.

Space is lacking for a full consideration of Professor Smith's attacks upon Kegan Paul's life of Godwin, Mrs. Julian Marshall's life of Mary Shelley, and Edward Dowden's life of Shelley. To him they are monuments to Lady Shelley's success in imposing her views upon her contemporaries and their successors. The first two are rather mediocre biographies of the Victorian "Life and Letters" type and have for many years been without any standing among Shelley scholars except as a source for otherwise inaccessible documents and records. Mary Shelley is charged with destroying certain documents of her father's that Paul (presumably) should have published, and Mrs. Marshall is charged with printing E. for C. in Mary's long letter about the Hoppner scandal, thus making Mary say that the nurse Elise, rather than Claire Clairmont, was ill at the time of the alleged birth of a child of Claire and Shelley. The first charge is nothing unless the importance of the suppressed documents can be established. No family is likely to turn over documents for publication without removing some of them, and Mary Shelley and Kegan Paul were more meticulous than most in stating not only the fact of destruction, but the general nature of the destroyed documents. The charge against Mrs. Marshall is true, and has been pointed out before (*Shelley*, II, 616). If Lady Shelley was responsible, however, why did she not omit from *Shelley and Mary* the corresponding printed entry, which remains to show that it was Claire who was ill?

Professor Dowden's biography of Shelley, on the other hand, really did have an important influence in transmitting an idea of the poet. It would require several pages, however, properly to modify the exaggerated charges made against Professor Dowden, and I shall not attempt it, though the materials are at hand. Since I have been quoted (and also misquoted and my meaning distorted) in criticism of him, I claim the privilege of adding some slight testimony. I have studied carefully every marginal note made by Professor Dowden in his copy of *Shelley and Mary* and I have followed him closely in his use of all of his basic materials. His use of his materials was scrupulous and exact, and I found no evidence of evasion or suppression. My reading of Dowden's biography and his letters confirms this opinion. He is not above criticism, but in my opinion he is one of the ablest biographers of his age.

*   *   *   *   *

Let us consider now the various arguments against the validity of current Shelley scholarship, on their merits as arguments, and without relation to the flimsy legend of which Professor Smith makes them a part. The whole body of Shelley scholarship, and most of the biographers individually, are charged with (1) accepting forged documents, (2) failing to use modern methods of investigation, (3) sentimental protectiveness, (4) unfairness to Harriet, (5) special pleading, and "lack of candor," (6) partial frustration by inability to gain access to important "vital documents." I shall consider most of these charges separately, and since I am myself the principal individual object of criticism among contemporary writers, I hereby put the reader on guard against any further "special pleading" or "lack of candor" of which I may be guilty in doing so.

(1) The examination of alleged forgeries is the most novel and sensational element in *The Shelley Legend*. The subject itself is not novel, for the alarm of forgery was thoroughly raised in 1852, in 1916-26, and again in 1927. Seymour De Ricci's *Bibliography of Shelley Letters* (1927), which furnishes the complete history of 600 of Shelley's letters, isolates and discusses forty-eight Major Byron forgeries of Shelley letters and raises a warning about another. So far as the number of Professor Smith's alleged forgeries can be added up (for he deploys the same ones repeatedly, like a stage army), he seems aware of about fifty Shelley letters attributable to Major Byron (pp. 58, 125), but mentions definitely only thirty-three or thirty-five (pp. 54, 78-80). This tallies pretty well with

De Ricci, who claims that the forty-eight he lists include all Major Byron forgeries of Shelley letters. De Ricci, therefore, actually warned Shelley scholars against more forgeries than Professor Smith does. Moreover, twenty-five of these letters were published in one volume in 1852 and have been known as forgeries for nearly a century.

Professor Smith considers only six alleged forgeries in detail, and only three of these are letters against which De Ricci had not long ago put Shelley scholars on guard. Two of the three happen to be Shelley's letter of January 17, 1817, to Byron, and Mary Shelley's letter of December 17, 1816, to Shelley. In Professor Smith's view, these letters *have* to be forgeries; otherwise they destroy his attack on Shelley's letter of December 15-16, 1816, which is his main exhibit both of forgeries innocently accepted by Shelley biographers, and of the family conspiracy against Harriet. For the letter to Byron refutes Professor Smith's claim that the "forged" letter of December 15-16, 1816, is the false basis for Shelley's alleged charges against Harriet; and the Mary Shelley letter completely validates the letter of December 15-16, being an answer to it. But *are* they forgeries, and what about the others?

At this point I should give my reasons, as fully as possible, for rejecting every single one of Professor Smith's six particular cases as forgeries in anything like a complete sense. There are individual weaknesses in each case, and there are general weaknesses covering most of the cases as a group. It would be a tedious business to make all the points that occur, and I shall omit some for the sake of brevity.

First as to the testimony of Professor Smith's professional handwriting expert, Mr. Louis Addison Waters. I cannot agree that professional testimony of this sort dwarfs into insignificance the testimony of scholars who are not professional handwriting experts, and I note with some amusement that

after Mr. Waters had examined his largest body of manuscripts (p. 40) he was in almost absolute agreement with the
independently-reached conclusions of two scholars, not pro-
fessionals, who had preceded him. If we establish confidence
in Mr. Waters by his agreement with non-professionals, we
also establish the competence of non-professional testimony
by its agreement with Mr. Waters. I have no desire to impugn
the competence of Mr. Waters, or even the correctness of most
of his conclusions—as far as they go. His services, as a matter
of fact, are much more talked about than actually used. One
sees a great display of some thirty illustrations of handwriting—and then realizes with surprise that in only two of the
six cases analyzed at length does Professor Smith make vis-
ible use of Mr. Waters' expert testimony. In all others he
is on the same footing as Mr. De Ricci, a man far more experienced with Shelley letters.

The manuscript of Shelley's *Proposal for Putting Reform
to the Vote* is condemned as a forgery on Mr. Waters' analysis
only. Since the genuineness of this manuscript has no bearing
on Shelley criticism or biography, because the *content* of the
document is admittedly genuine, it may be dismissed briefly
(omitting several errors in the supporting argument on pp.
290-295) by observing that it has an unimpeached provenance
going back to Ollier, Shelley's publisher. In essence the argument is that this provenance must be fraudulent because
the handwriting is fraudulent. But as long as the ownership
of this document until 1879 by the Ollier family is admitted
it is impossible to show, or even imagine, (1) how a forger
could plant it in their possession, and (2) why he would do
so, when they admittedly possessed the genuine original.

The second case (Shelley's letter of December 15-16, 1816)
in which expert testimony is employed is far more important;
it is in fact almost the keystone of the book. Professor Smith
ties to it his case against three other letters out of the five

which he examines in detail, and he also bases largely on this combined attack both (1) his contention that the Shelley family deliberately promoted fraudulent charges against Harriet's character and (2) his contention that Shelley himself never made the statements which these letters contain.

This letter is attacked on the basis both of handwriting and of doubtful provenance. Mr. Waters is sure the handwriting is forged, and Professor Smith cites evidence to show that the history of the manuscript is doubtful and leads straight back to Major Byron, the forger. The case seems to be closed, and it *is* closed, so far as most or all of the manuscripts are concerned. It is never safe, however, to conclude that because a manuscript is false its contents are also false. There are four manuscripts of this letter. Three of them must be false, and the fourth may be. De Ricci long ago noted the doubtful nature and antecedents of three of them. Lady Shelley, at the same time that she denounced one of the manuscripts as a forgery, claimed that she possessed the genuine original of which it was a copy. Professor Smith may be right in claiming this genuine original has never been produced. Yet it is well known that the forger actually possessed or had the use of some genuine originals; it is also known that some of Major Byron's forgeries are copies of genuine originals; and there is a strong presumption that wherever he has produced a number of identical or closely similar forgeries there probably was a genuine original to account for the identity. Any clever forger would know that it is far more difficult to forge facts than to forge handwriting.

We need not depend upon such probabilities, however, for Mary Shelley validated this letter by answering it on December 17, 1816. Unless her answer is a forgery—the first Mary Shelley forgery on record—then there was a genuine letter which Mr. Waters has never examined, or which he has examined and been mistaken about. To biography and criticism it makes no difference which, if any, of the slightly variant versions she was answering.

Professor Smith's answer to this crushing fact is the only possible one for his case. Mary's validating letter must be abolished if the whole structure built up around Shelley's December 15-16, 1816, letter is to be saved from complete collapse. After calling attention to two trifling variations between Dowden's printed text of this letter and the manuscript in the Bodleian Library (such variations as commonly occur when genuine manuscripts are copied inaccurately) Professor Smith concludes that "the authenticity of this letter may remain suspect" until examination proves the handwriting to be either Mary's or Major Byron's; and, if Mary's, whether she wrote it in 1816 or 1845-50.

This is to suggest that Mary either forged or procured the forgery of her own letter, in order to validate a previous forgery. If she did this, why did she not also validate in the same way Shelley's allegedly forged letters of January 11 and January 17, both of which support the "Harriet Scandal"? Why one without the others, when all were needed? The argument is totally absurd, and even so, it rests entirely on the assumption of Mary's guilty connivance with a forger, which in turn has no definite basis except suspicion of her general character.

Shelley's letter of January 11, 1817, to Mary supports his attitude toward Harriet as expressed in the December 15-16 letter, and so is naturally suspect to Professor Smith. His letter of January 17, 1817, to Byron also supports a charge against Harriet's sister Eliza that occurs in the December 15-16 letter; and so both letters would support the genuineness of the December 15-16 letter—unless they can be proved to be forgeries. Without the use of Mr. Waters' handwriting analysis Professor Smith pronounces both of them forgeries. The first exists in four variants, at least three of which *must* be forgeries, and there is a broad trail to the door of Major

Byron. Yet we must remember that the Major admittedly had some genuine manuscripts either begged, borrowed, or stolen, that some of his forgeries are copies of genuine originals (which would be more likely in the case of multiple versions), and that the letter here under suspicion is cut out of the same cloth as the suspected letter which Mary's answering letter validates. It would seem probable, therefore, either that one of the four versions of this letter is genuine or that all come from a genuine original not now in evidence.

As for the letter to Byron, it supports the attack on Eliza Westbrook in the December 15-16 letter, and so the two are to that extent reciprocally supported. It is accused as a forgery on two grounds: because the version in *Shelley and Mary* is said to vary in part of one sentence from the versions as printed in *Lord Byron's Correspondence* and in the Julian edition of Shelley's letters; and also because there are two or three slight irregularities in the salutation and address similar to irregularities in Major Byron's forgeries. Both points are fairly common with genuine letters, and so are no evidence of forgery. Professor Smith then proves that Hobhouse, who owned the manuscript, *could* have got it directly or indirectly from the forger (because, like several million others, he was once in London at the same time!) without the slightest indication, either direct or presumptive, that he actually *did*. In fact, the "inexplicable addition" (p. 130) of part of a sentence in *Shelley and Mary* merely proves that Lady Shelley, the chief suspect, was the only person who handled this letter accurately. *Lord Byron's Correspondence* (1922), at least in the first two printings, omitted the part sentence, and this error was repeated in the Julian edition (1926), which is based on *Lord Byron's Correspondence*. Obviously there were never any grounds for suspecting this letter, except that Professor Smith's erroneous thesis required it. Yet Professor Smith, on no grounds at all, without examining the manuscript, calmly calls it (p. 131) a Major Byron forgery! This is the sheer anarchy of all scholarship and intellectual honesty.

*   *   *   *   *

Thus far I have dealt with the forgery alarm on the basis of Professor Smith's belief that proved forgeries constitute a serious danger to Shelley biography; and I have shown that even on this basis the charges break down completely. I now offer the suggestion that the basis itself is a totally naïve and unscholarly assumption. Throughout their whole book it never occurs to the authors to draw an absolutely fundamental distinction between two kinds of forgery. Ordinary commercial forgery has for its primary object the establishment of a false statement as truth—a signature to a will, a date, or a clause. The forgery of handwriting is only an incidental means to this end. Modern literary forgery has for its primary object the establishment of a manuscript as genuine, so that it may be sold to collectors. The content of the manuscript is unimportant to the forger, except that it must not subject the document to challenge. The forger's object is to avoid the scholar as far as possible, for fear of detection by someone who knows the facts better than himself. Thus it is that modern forged literary documents are either copies of genuine material or else they are so neuter in content as to risk no challenge from scholars. Proof of this is glaringly apparent in the Major Byron forgeries. Some are copies and some are composites, and all but the copies are completely neuter in their content. The forger was risking nothing unnecessarily. This fact is clearly evident in the twenty-five forged letters published in 1852, which are analyzed in this volume (pp. 58-62) with absolutely no perception of the most important fact that they demonstrate—namely, that they could be of no possible use to Shelley biography even if they were genuine. Two of the twenty-five (p. 61) are admittedly copies of letters whose genuineness is not contested. Only four are found to be completely non-Shelleyan in content. The same worthlessness to biography is true of the 1916-1926 forgeries discussed on pages 297-300. If all the scores and hundreds of undetected forgeries alluded to actually existed, it would be equally true of them. Our experts on forgery have simply missed the most important and the most obvious point about its bearing on biography. They could still have been protected from utter absurdity had they not missed another equally obvious point, namely, that Seymour De Ricci's detailed history of the six hundred most important Shelley letters afforded a protection against forgers enjoyed by the biographers of no other important English poet—even though the protection, as we have seen—was needed only by collectors of manuscripts.

Four out of the five letters which Professor Smith undertakes to prove are forgeries deal with Shelley's charges against Harriet and her sister. He claims more than once[2] (pp. 84, 124, 260) that they are the sole evidence that Shelley ever uttered such charges, and he hints broadly again and again that the "forged" letters were manufactured to support the charges. Unfortunately, however, the charges are no more limited to these letters than the letters themselves are forged.

There exist at least six contradictions of the statement that the Harriet charges depend solely on these "forged" letters. There are the account of her suicide in the *Times*, stating that she was pregnant, and the testimony at the coroner's inquest, to the same effect. There is Shelley's letter to Southey (quoted in *Shelley*, II, 199) which hints pretty clearly at similar

[2] Professor Smith's language straddles on this point, but his meaning is clear enough. On p. 84 it is "a single paragraph" in the letter of December 15-16, 1816, on which the charges against Harriet depend. On p. 124 the charges "depend solely upon Godwin's and Mary's allegations and upon the forged letters of December 16, January 11, and January 17."

charges. There is Southey's answer, so definite that Southey could not have based it on Shelley's letter: ". . . she followed your example as faithfully as your lessons, and . . . the catastrophe was produced by shame. You robbed her of her moral and religious principles. . . ." etc. (*Correspondence of Robert Southey with Caroline Bowles*, p. 364). There is a letter written by Charles Brown in Italy in 1825, quoted by Professor Smith himself (p. 27), which tells the story of Harriet and Shelley as Brown got it from Hunt and another friend of Shelley: "After a time her conduct was such that her infidelities were scarcely the worst part . . ." etc. To this should be added a sixth item which Professor Smith also unwittingly records (p. 202), namely, that George Henry Lewes, in his early researches, was told by Hunt and others that after the separation Harriet took up with another man, and later with anyone. This was long before the forgeries episode.

*   *   *   *   *

Most of Professor Smith's remaining charges against Shelley scholarship may be answered more briefly.

(2) By "failure to use modern means of investigation" he probably means professional handwriting investigation. I have just shown why such an investigation was deemed unnecessary for biography in the five letters which he himself examines—only one of them, by the way, with a handwriting analysis. In examining crossed-out passages in Claire Clairmont's journal I used infra-red photography, photographic enlargements, stereopticon projection, and the experience of handwriting experts in the U. S. Signal Corps. For some of this there is plain evidence in my *Shelley* (II, 570).

(3) The charge of sentimental protectiveness concerns partly the Harriet matter, but goes far beyond. Virtually all biographers and editors, beginning with Dowden, are charged with protecting Shelley by playing down his loves for other

women, particularly Claire Clairmont. The present writer, in addition, is charged with sentimentalizing, glossing over, and fundamentally distorting two newly-discovered episodes, namely, the affair between Hogg and Mary in 1815, and the "Hoppner Scandal" concerning Shelley's Neapolitan ward. In a word, Shelley biographers and scholars are charged with having, for over a century, promoted a radically false notion of the poet's character. The charge is the more remarkable in that it is supported by no single scrap of fresh evidence—all the ammunition that Professor Smith uses comes from the lockers of those against whom he uses it.

What we have here is, from one point of view, no more than a simple and legitimate difference of opinion on three points, on none of which has any Shelley biographer ever pretended to a final and absolute conclusion. Professor Smith is entitled to disagree, but he is hardly entitled to stigmatize others as "sentimentally protective" and "not candid," merely because they do not agree with him. Serious scholars cannot be tried by adjectives and epithets imputing discreditable motives for which there is no evidence. Since Professor Smith has no new facts to offer on any of the three points at issue, the probable truth remains a matter of opinion, but Professor Smith still lies open to criticism for his misuse and distortion of the facts commonly known.

Underlying his whole treatment of Shelley's relations with women is his complete distortion of what Shelley meant by the word love. He seems entirely ignorant of the profound and obvious effect on Shelley's mind and expression of the Platonic, Petrarchan, and Dantean conceptions of love. Having entered upon a re-interpretation of Shelley's character while scorning the use of his works for understanding him (p. 305), he nevertheless does use the works when it suits his purpose; e.g., he quotes (p. 160) without identification or date two lines written in December 1818 as if they were the immediate expression of a feeling two years earlier in utterly different circumstances, and he quotes and cites the "True love" passage from *Epipsychidion* as if it were a justification of the common notion of "free love" as free sexual union—although the poem itself, and all Shelley's mature utterances on the subject, completely refute the idea. He perverts Hogg's testimony on the subject by saying that he hints of Shelley's numerous "conquests of women" and neglecting to explain that Hogg's context makes it plain these were only sentimental affairs, in the spirit of Wieland's novels, and without quoting Hogg's explicit testimony to the purity of Shelley's mind and conduct in sexual matters. He says (p. 3) that Shelley "believed in and practiced free love throughout his life" without apparently the slightest knowledge of Shelley's explicit denial of a similar charge in his letter of May 26, 1820, to Byron. To him, in spite of all Shelley's testimony to the contrary, Shelley's notion of love is (p. 208) an "incessant quest for the divine moment of perfect passion." It is in this sense, apparently, that he expects his readers to understand Shelley's use of the word every time it is quoted. He takes no note of the fact that in letters and poems to most of these women he is supposed to love with "passion" Shelley carefully and tactfully stated that his love was not the usual physical passion—and I have pointed out this fact specifically in the cases of Elizabeth Hitchener, Emilia Viviani, Sophia Stacey, and the unknown recipient (Jane Williams?) of "One Word is Too Often Profaned," a poem which clearly states the distinction Shelley made habitually.

There are many factual distortions in the treatment of Claire and Shelley, particularly exaggerations and unwarranted conclusions about quarrels and Shelley's absences from home. One such absence is represented as a temporary desertion of Mary to take a trip of unspecified duration with Claire. It was in fact a hurried visit to Field Place made necessary by his grandfather's death; it lasted probably one or two days and not possibly more than five; and Claire accompanied Shelley because Mary was still too ill to do so, and wrote to Mary during the absence. Professor Smith makes much of these absences by frequent dark allusions, and on page 160 claims without proof that in July 1816 Shelley was absent from Mary "more than a month." Yet on the very next page he quotes Mary's letter of January 17, 1817, which seems to show that previous to that time Shelley had *never* been absent from Mary as much as eleven days. Here Mary says, "never before have you been so long away"—and Shelley had left her only eleven days before. Mary is referred to several times as having initiated a "pursuit" of Hogg, yet her first letter, quoted on page 148, indicates pretty clearly that Hogg was the initiator: "You love me, you say—I wish I could return it with the passion you deserve. . . ." At the end of another paragraph containing several other distortions (p. 158) Professor Smith refers the reader, evidently for further details of the Mary-Hogg affair, to *Shelley and Mary*, I, 48-69. Since most readers can never check this reference, I refer them to a summary of the pages in my *Shelley* (I, 388-389) showing that they deal with the first acquaintance of Mary and Hogg and have no bearing on their "affair."

The climax of absurdity is reached in this particular series of misrepresentations when a garbled quotation from Mary's journal of February 28, 1819, is offered as a proof, first that there were violent quarrels at the time between Mary and Claire, and, second, that Mary was a liar. The entry reads: "Leave Naples at two [not three] o'clock. Sleep at Capua. Vincenzo drives.—A most tremendous fuss." It is inaccurately quoted on page 241, though "fuss" is quoted correctly in the singular. But "fuss" had previously been pluralized as "tremendous fusses" to prove "by Mary's own words" the commonness of serious quarrels; and a little later (p. 242) is proof that Mary lied to Mrs. Hoppner in claiming friendly relations with Claire. Any Englishman and any dictionary could have told Professor Smith that this passage could not possibly mean anything except that there was considerable last-minute hurry and confusion in the departure from Naples or the arrival at Capua. The characters of two dead women are assailed because Professor Smith (1) cannot read a diary without reading his own preconceptions into it, (2) cannot quote it twice without garbling twice, and (3) cannot understand a common English phrase. This is the scholarship offered—and subsequently endorsed by reputable publishers and reviewers—to supplant most previous scholarship on the subject.

Many more examples of similar error, ignorance, and distortion could be established, if space permitted, but I will here cite only two, both concerned with the misrepresentation of documents. In taking up the old argument that Fanny Godwin and Shelley were lovers Professor Smith quotes Shelley's poem generally supposed to have been written about Fanny's suicide (p. 217), which is in itself no evidence at all of a love affair. He then quotes, as Shelley's note on the back of the manuscript, "It is not my fault. It is not to be alluded to." One makes two interesting discoveries, however, when this quotation is checked against its source. The same manuscript page contains part of a poem written over two years later on the death of Shelley's son William. The note on the back is in the plural. "These cannot be forgotten. It is not my fault—it is not to be alluded to." Thus by garbled quotation a statement intended to apply immediately and mainly to the death of William Shelley is made to apply exclusively to Fanny Godwin.

Skipping a number of other errors (for who can have the patience to attack individually every gnat in a swarm?) we come to a somewhat similar misuse of document in the Hogg-

Mary affair. Professor Smith refers to my account of this as "fragmentary" (p. 146), presumably because I summarize, rather than quote directly, the letters of Mary to Hogg. However, I summarized all the facts of any significance, and refrained from quoting directly only out of consideration for the wishes of Professor Gordon, whose unpublished book was my source. Professor Smith then states that Professor Gordon's book, when published entire, will considerably alter the "Shelley legend." He quotes what he calls "a few" of Mary's letters in this affair. Actually his "few" are all but two, and those two are short unemotional notes probably omitted because of no value to his argument. Everything of importance in the *Shelley Letters* of Professor Gordon has already been published, by myself in summary, and by direct quotation both by Professor Smith and by the Golden Cockerel Press in England. Professor Smith's references to further materials in the *Shelley Letters* are false and misleading.

(4) The charge of unfairness to Harriet depends mainly on the alleged "forged" letters containing Shelley's charges, and is largely dissipated when the extent of Professor Smith's errors, exaggerations, and false conclusions concerning these documents is clear.

(5) We return now to the last of Professor Smith's charges against Shelley biography in general, for I think "lack of candor, and special pleading" has already been sufficiently noticed in dealing with other subjects, and it is perhaps beside the point to expose more than has already appeared incidentally, in his misuse of facts and document his own "lack of candor."

(6) Professor Smith asserts that the biography of Shelley has been frustrated by the destruction of materials and by inability to gain access to important "vital" documents. Probably every biographer who ever wrote finds that some documents have been lost, destroyed, or mutilated. Yet it is

certainly incontestable that for Shelley's biography more important documents are available than for most English poets, and that this is due rather largely to the two women whom Professor Smith berates. Undoubtedly, we would possess more detailed knowledge of the Shelley domestic menage in 1815 if a number of excisions had not been made in the journal. But the excisions do not conceal the *fact* of some domestic friction connected with Claire, nor is it at all clear that some of them at this time were not to protect Peacock's mysterious love affair. In any event the excisions throughout the whole journal are relatively infrequent and very probably of relative unimportance. Anyone at all acquainted with the journals of Mary and Claire perceives early that both were too circumspect as diarists ever to write down much that would later need to be excised for really serious reasons.

Certainly Professor Smith greatly exaggerates his point about "vital Shelley source materials . . . still withheld from examination" (p. 303). Let us consider the materials he cites: (1) "Many Mary Shelley letters"—virtually all such letters are post-Shelleyan, and biographically insignificant. (2) "original ms. journals of Shelley and Mary and Claire"—The Shelley-Mary journals have been used in manuscript by Dowden. Miss R. Glynn Grylls has had unimpeded access to the manuscript for herself, and has checked some points in it for me; also A. Koszul probably had access to it in his *La jeunesse de Shelley*. Claire's manuscript journals were for years available in Mr. Wise's library; photostats of them have been for some years available in the Duke University Library. (4) "the Major Byron forgeries"—most of these were immediately detected, half of those known have been in print for nearly a century, and I have shown that they have no biographical significance. (5) "William Godwin's diaries"— They were freely used and quoted by Kegan Paul and Dowden and have since been accessible to Miss Grylls. (6) "Other (compiled) journals, still withheld"—This is too vague for comment—I know of none.

The reckless ignorance and inaccuracy of Professor Smith's statement speaks for itself on the subject of his general reliability. As for the Shelley biographers, it is evident that they could not have been seriously crippled by lack of access to materials almost all of which some of them actually used.

*   *   *   *   *

Thus far I have analyzed *The Shelley Legend* strictly from the point of view of its leading theses—the so-called Shelley "legend," the "forgeries," and the alleged untrustworthiness of the whole body of Shelley scholarship, which is charged with substituting legend for the "real" Shelley. I have considered these points carefully, with a seriousness unmerited either by the intrinsic absurdity of the book or by the manners of its authors; and I have shown the worthlessness of these leading ideas. There are times, however, when politeness is excessive and may even obscure the real point. Over and beyond the fallacy of Professor Smith's general ideas, the astonishing presumptuousness and ignorance of this book may easily be demonstrated by considering two points which I have so far neglected. These points are (1) the author's fitness for the special task in hand and (2) the general quality of scholarly competence and integrity shown by the book.

(1) If Professor Smith is to substitute his own radically different interpretation of Shelley for one confirmed by dozens of able writers in various countries through a century of effort and study, it stands to reason that he must know something about Shelley. He may be given credit for this either by previous achievement or by the present one—and preferably by both—but lacking such credit, his book is very apt to prove something entirely unintended. To what extent,

then, does Professor Smith possess any consistent, substantial view of Shelley?

We need not emphasize too strongly the fact that Professor Smith and his young associates are all absolute novices in the field of scholarship they are attempting to overturn—David also was a newcomer. Professor Smith does intimate in his Preface a dependence upon "the large store of knowledge about Shelley and his circle" possessed by one of his associates (a recent graduate student at Lehigh University), but this claim must be validated by the book, which is the only real evidence available. The Preface also acknowledges "valuable criticisms of the text" by Messrs. John Carter and David A. Randall, of Scribner's Rare Book Department—excellent scholars, perhaps, but not authorities on Shelley. Shelley scholars were consulted, as I was, on particular points, but I suppose the others, like myself, were kept ignorant of the real nature of the book. The wonder is that Professor Smith, with these limitations of background, chose for his adventure such an intricate and unfamiliar field as that of Shelley scholarship.

So much for the previous record; what evidence of special fitness is furnished by the book itself? In the Preface we are told that this book is not directed against Shelley, but against those who have distorted his biography. In the end (p. 306) we are told that nothing can "ever dim the love of his generous but prodigal spirit or the luster of his poetry" (see also p. 305); and earlier (p. 212) that his "lyrical gifts" will "glorify the Shelley name forever." Just what sort of "generous spirit" this is we learn from a number of pejorative quotations such as Aldous Huxley's attack in *Point Counter Point* (quoted with approval, p. 302), from the repeated assertion that he ruined the lives of several women, from a reference to Jeaffreson's catalogue of thirty-one Shelley "lies" (p. 254), and from the fact that Shelley is "an adulterer" (p. 171). The principal evidence for Shelley's poetic "lustre" and "glory" occurs on page 211 with a passing mention of "Shelley's habit of pouring forth meaningless onomatopoeia with an increasing ecstasy," and a statement (p. 266) that "Shelley made up his unnatural forests as he went along." To this may be added the total misconception, previously noted, of Shelley's attitude toward love in theory and practice, and the confusion indicated by twice calling my *Shelley* a "great" book in the Preface while thoroughly damning its shorter version on page 261.

This may not be quite all, but it is nearly all, and truly representative. We need not argue the justice or injustice of any of these terms; we need only point out that taken together at face value, they indicate a superficial, confused, hasty, and uncoordinated notion of both biography and criticism. Professor Smith's disagreement with the Shelley accepted by critics and biographers for over a century evidently depends not on a well-founded, integrated concept of Shelley's character and poetry, but upon hasty impulse, recklessly and ignorantly expressed.

(2) We now turn from the lack of a respectable conception of the central character to the evidence of general scholarly proficiency furnished by the volume—the accuracy and scope of detail, and the integrity, fairness, and logic of presentation without which no book can pretend to scholarship. To anyone at all familiar with the Shelleyan background the book abounds in all sorts of errors. I have noted over two hundred of them—misstatements, half-statements, incomplete conclusions, contradictions, circular arguments, misuse of documents, unproved, doubtful, or false assumptions, etc., etc. Some of them are repetitions—to the extent that the book itself is repetitious—and some have been used earlier in this paper. Others must remain unpublished for lack of space, but I quote some samples in the following paragraphs.

On page 1 we are told that Claire Clairmont captivated

Byron in order to get a more famous poet than Shelley, that Claire had "always loved" Shelley, and that she "never loved" Byron—all without evidence, either on page 1 or later. There is no known evidence to support any of the three statements except an interview with Claire in her old age in which she is said to have admitted that she loved Shelley.

On page 2, "Shelley in several letters was moved to express great annoyance at his wife's continual prying into his letters." No references are given. There are no letters expressing great annoyance and no letters indicating that Mary pried into his correspondence. This statement is probably an exaggeration of a passage in a letter to Claire referring to Mary's being at his side as he wrote, and another letter in which Claire is told that Mary does *not* see her correspondence. On the same page we learn that "Mary's quarrels with Medwin, Byron, Guiccioli, and others of the Italian group made Shelley's last years an intermittent hell." Here we have two statements that are absolutely false, so far as any discoverable evidence is concerned. Shelley had moments of dejection connected with Mary, but his poems and letters countenance no such wild statement as "intermittent hell." Also there is no proof of the alleged quarrels with others; indeed, Professor Smith later (p. 26) quotes a letter of Trelawny blaming Mary for *not* quarreling with Medwin in Italy.

On page 3 we are told that Shelley never repudiated Godwin's antimatrimonial thesis. We are given a denunciation of marriage written at the age of nineteen, and are *not* reminded that afterwards Shelley was married three times (twice to Harriet). We are told also that he believed in and practiced free love all his life—when there is no tangible evidence that he *ever* practiced it—and we get in proof a quotation from *Epipsychidion* that only proves Professor Smith's misunderstanding of Shelley and the poem. We get no mention of Shelley's letter to Byron on the desirability of teaching chastity to girls. We learn also that both Harriet and Mary insisted on marriage to Shelley, when there is no evidence at all in either case and some evidence to the contrary in Harriet's. On the same page we are told that the family's attempts "to suppress the record" prove Shelley's lifelong belief and practice of free love. Such efforts could prove nothing about Shelley; they could not even prove the family's belief about Shelley unless we knew exactly what was suppressed, and why.

So much, yet not quite all, for the first three pages—and we could plow ahead in the same manner for the rest of the book and fill perhaps forty pages with corrections. Hereafter we must take longer jumps.

No evidence is given or can be given that there was a falling out between Mary and Hogg in April, 1815 (p. 9); Shelley's interest in the Gisbornes did not succeed his interest in Sophia Stacey (p. 10), but preceded it by seventeen months. Mary Shelley did not suppress passages and names in her 1840 republication of *History of a Six Weeks' Tour* in the sense that Professor Smith implies (p. 28). There was nothing important to suppress. Professor Smith is the real suppressor in failing to mention that this book was first published anonymously in 1817, when names and incidents were suppressed simply from literary convention, without ulterior motive. No proved forgeries of Shelley letters have crept back into Shelley biography as genuine (as charged on p. 64); in fact, I know of only one proved (?) forgery that ever entered the biographies; and that was immediately expelled. Hogg's attempted seduction of Harriet occurred in York, not Edinburgh (as twice stated, pp. 153, 154). If Elizabeth Hitchener's motives toward Shelley were "primarily mercenary" (p. 154), oughtn't it to be mentioned that Shelley borrowed money from her and died in her debt? If Lady Shelley is to be charged with suppression because she does not mention Elizabeth Hitchener in *Shelley Memorials* (p. 185), oughtn't it to be mentioned that *Shelley Memorials* was written ten years before the Elizabeth Hitchener correspondence was known to the first scholar and twenty-three years before any of it was printed with her name?

It is false to say (p. 216) that "Professor White merely accepts the testimony of Paul and Mrs. Marshall" that Fanny Imlay was not in love with Shelley when my text shows (I, 719) that I examined all available evidence. It is false to say that the scandalous story believed of Shelley and Claire Clairmont by the Hoppners was "the scandal of the London drawing rooms at the time" (p. 223), and (p. 228) that it caused "the moral backfire from Southey, from the *Literary Gazette*, and other periodicals." There is no evidence that the story was even known in England beyond what Shelley thought might be a possible veiled reference to it in the *Literary Gazette*. Southey's "moral backfire" was provoked by a challenging letter from Shelley. It is ridiculous to wonder why Shelley's biographers, apropos of Fanny Imlay's suicide, have not explained Shelley's presence in Bristol on September 30, 1816 (p. 218). Considering that Bristol and Bath are neighboring towns, Shelley's presence there on any particular day requires no more explanation than the presence of a Princetonian in New York—and had Professor Smith checked his dates, he would have seen that Fanny Imlay was in London at the time. It is also ridiculous to claim that Miss Grylls contradicts herself (p. 224) by saying both that Claire Clairmont was not in love with Shelley, and that she was "genuinely fond" of him—but it is at least consistent, for in this book there seems to be no place for any affection short of, or beyond, physical passion.

Again and again in his letters Byron refers to Allegra, his child by Claire Clairmont, as his natural daughter. But Professor Smith tells us more than once (p. 230, etc.) that Byron was plagued with doubts. He cites as evidence (p. 234) Byron's obviously teasing remark to the child's nurse that Allegra was "Mr. Shelley's child." The fact that Claire Clairmont is the source of this quotation is the best possible proof that its meaning could not have been serious. Shelley's very important unsigned letter telling Mary about the Hoppner Scandal is treated as suspicious because of "the strangely missing last paragraphs" (pp. 231-233). Apparently this is another one of those criminal suppressions by the Shelley family. But the suppression, if anybody's, is Professor Smith's, for Shelley's very next letter to Mary proves that this letter is complete. It refers to the Hoppner story in this letter as "the latter half of it." This statement is true of the letter as it stands, and could not be true if there were any missing paragraphs at the end. Mr. T. J. Wise (a favorite stalking-horse) is subjected to dark suspicion (p. 294) in connection with Schultess-Young's publication of some of Major Byron's forged letters. The fact that Mr. Wise called them forgeries in his *Bibliography of Byron* makes no difference and is not mentioned. And the evidence?—Mr. Wise and Mr. Young were once neighbors in Hampstead! Even the Third Commandment visits upon others only "the sins of the fathers," but Professor Smith's logic would make an equal curse of the neighbors.

A few scattered gems may be offered about Shelley himself. A section headed "Shelley's Reputation in England" (pp. 13-14) is limited to three unfavorable quotations, ignoring entirely the large mass of favorable comment in my *The Unextinguished Hearth* (1938) and ignoring also the favorable testimony of many individuals who knew and liked Shelley. Later (p. 234) it is asserted that the Shelleys were driven from Marlow by scandal. No evidence is cited, and none exists. On the contrary, Peacock's memoirs and the correspondence of the Shelleys show very clearly the real reasons for departure. Finally, Shelley is charged with loving Claire more than Mary, and Allegra more than his own children (p. 224). This is based upon one sentence in a letter that was written to apply to a particular moment only, and is nothing but common sense in that situation—"Our first thought [in this particular emergency] should be Allegra—Our second our own plans." By the same sort of reasoning Richard III preferred the company of horses to that of the peers of England, because he once said, "My kingdom for a horse."

*   *   *   *   *

In the end, what have we? (1) An exhumation of Harriet Shelley to receive a resounding "vindication," more quietly accorded her by common consent of Shelleyans for the last thirty or forty years.

(2) A re-affirmation of Jeaffreson's attacks on Mary and Lady Shelley, supported mainly by suspicion, and demonstrably false in some of their alleged factual support. This "warning" to unwary Shelleyans has been available to them, in its main features, since Jeaffreson uttered it, over sixty years ago.

(3) A hurly-burly about forged documents, amounting to less than seventy-five that are known, only five or six of which could have had any possible biographical significance, and those five or six not proved to be forgeries except in certain copies—with strong indications that the contents are genuine. This is supposed to be a "warning" to scholars who had known about these forgeries much longer than Professor Smith, since Mr. De Ricci listed in 1927 all of the Major Byron Shelley forgeries for which any real evidence can be offered.

(4) A charge, based on this stale information, that every one of the six or seven hundred Shelley letters (and why not the added two thousand or more written by Mary and Byron?) is suspect until the handwriting is guaranteed—this in spite of

the fact that the history of Shelley letters is better known than that of almost any other author, and that the known forgeries are so generally neuter in nature that even if genuine, their effect on Shelley biography would be a small fraction of one per cent. (Professor Smith, of course, confidently uses many such letters himself, submitting only a very few to analysis.)

(5) A violent attack on all Shelley biographers for presenting a fundamentally false picture of the poet. This attack is supported by no evidence not previously available to the biographers, is based upon a background of unfamiliarity with the subject, and is advanced with more factual errors, exaggerations, and distortions than the present writer has ever before encountered in any printed book.

The Shelley Legend[1]

Frederick L. Jones

L ATE IN 1945 appeared a book entitled *The Shelley Legend*. It was published by Charles Scribner's Sons, and was
written by Professor Robert M. Smith of Lehigh University
in collaboration with Mr. Theodore G. Ehrsam, Miss Martha
M. Schlegel, and Mr. Louis A. Waters. These authors began
their labors in 1943 with apparently no previous experience in
Shelley research and in less than two years claim to have
discovered not only the real Shelley but also the fact that the
patient biographical and critical labors of a long line of predecessors are in the main wrong. They even "venture the opinion
that at least fifty per cent of the present attitude toward
Shelley still stems from this [Lady Shelley's] cult of wor-
shippers" (p. 305). Their predecessors include Leigh Hunt,
Mary Shelley, Thomas Medwin, T. J. Hogg, T. L. Peacock,
E. J. Trelawny, Lady Jane Shelley, Richard Garnett, D. F.
MacCarthy, W. M. Rossetti, H. Buxton Forman, J. Cordy
Jeaffreson, Edward Dowden, Mrs. Julian Marshall, J. A.
Symonds, William Sharpe, A. J. Koszul, Mrs. Helen Rossetti
Angeli, Walter Peck, André Maurois, Newman I. White, and
a host of lesser contributors, many of whom are of the highest
intellectual and scholarly attainments. It is claimed that these

[1] Originally published in *Publications of the Modern Modern Language
Association* (LXI, September 1946, 848-890), and reprinted here by permission of the Editor.—Permission to quote from *The Shelley Legend* has
been granted by the Publisher, Charles Scribner's Sons.

intelligent people, who have accumulated, tested, and published the greatest quantity of materials on any modern writer, have lacked discernment sufficient to free themselves from a false interpretation of Shelley presented to the world by Mary Shelley and Lady Jane Shelley and have been unable to base their conclusions on the facts in hand. This claim is made in spite of the fact, evident from the book itself, that no authors in question except Richard Garnett, Dowden, and Mrs. Marshall can in any way be shown as coming within the sphere of Lady Shelley's influence, and in spite of the fact that some were positive rebels against any possible influence of Lady Shelley; namely, Peacock, Trelawny, W. M. Rossetti, and J. Cordy Jeaffreson.

We are invited to "see Shelley plain," as the authors of *The Shelley Legend* see him. It is a little difficult to get from them definite statements as to what the real Shelley is, but certainly the main theme is the constantly repeated idea that Shelley was one who "believed in and practiced free love throughout his life, his poetic version of his passionate creed . . . [being]: 'True Love in this differs from gold and clay / That to divide is not to take away' " (p. 3). Shelley's letter of December 11, 1821, to Claire is therefore interpreted "as a forthright statement of his real need, physically and spiritually, for Claire" (p. 18). Frances Winwar, who is quoted on p. 134, expresses the idea much better: "I wonder why Shelley biographers play the cuttlefish with Shelley and his women—Claire, Sophia, Jane Williams? Why do they not accept the man for what he was—one who found in the physical act of love the sum and culmination of spiritual yearnings—however much he might sublimate his experiences in poetry." Occasionally we are reminded that Shelley was "the radiant poet . . . the impetuous and generous creature of pure fire and spirit who irresistibly captured the love and esteem of many men and women"; but generally emphasized is "the other Shelley whose kiss was as the kiss of death and whose touch in the real world was a whirlwind of devastation, upsetting the life of nearly everyone with whom it came into contact and leaving an appalling trail of acrimonious litigation, financial chaos, childbirth and death, double suicide and disaster behind him" (p. 2).

I do not believe that the authors have revealed the elusive Shelley any better than a score of earlier writers, and not nearly so well as many other writers. Nor does it concern me that they defend Harriet, abuse Mary and Lady Shelley, magnify Claire as Shelley's lover, and believe the Hoppner story. All this is old in Shelley scholarship and has been done more effectively. Peacock has been Harriet's knight errant; Trelawny and Massingham are better detractors of Mary; Mrs. Angeli and Newman White have given incomparably better accounts of Mary and Shelley's differences during Shelley's last years; Trelawny, Jeaffreson, and many others have dealt harshly with Lady Shelley; the tale of Shelley and Claire as lovers has existed in a variety of forms since 1814, Shelley himself having written on August 7, 1821 to Mary: "Elise says [to the Hoppners] that Clare was my mistress; that is all very well and so far there is nothing new: all the world has heard so much, and people may believe or not believe as they think good."[2] The Hoppner story has been debated often and has been believed by more than one person before these authors, who though they confess that "the evidences . . . are by no means conclusive" (p. 18), assume throughout their book that the case is proved. In fact, J. Cordy Jeaffreson's *The Real Shelley* (1885), of which *The Shelley Legend* is a direct descendant, is a much more vigorous, sys-

[2] *The Complete Works of P. B. Shelley*, ed. Roger Ingpen and Walter E. Peck. 10 vols. Published for the Julian Editions (London and New York, 1926-29), x, 298.—All references to Shelley's letters are to the Julian Edition. References to Mary's letters are to *The Letters of Mary W. Shelley*, collected and edited by Frederick L. Jones, 2 vols. (Norman: Oklahoma University Press, 1944).

tematic, and readable book. It at least gives a straightforward, clear-cut view of Shelley as a liar with a turned-up nose.

Nor does it greatly concern me that popular reviews have on the whole spoken favorably of *The Shelley Legend* as "a breath of fresh air" and as other desirable things in Shelley scholarship. The ignorance of the reviewers and their enjoyment of the shocking and sensational elements have, however, led them uncritically to endorse two unproved charges which strike at the very foundation of Shelley scholarship. It is these charges alone which concern me, for if they are not refuted they can lead to endless error. *The Shelley Legend* will eventually sink to its place beside Jeaffreson's little-used *Real Shelley*, but it would be well to hasten the process.

I propose therefore to examine *The Shelley Legend* systematically with reference to important matters and to demonstrate that the only contentions of any importance are not true, and that the authors are guilty of so many inaccuracies that a reader must be chary of accepting any of their facts or statements without checking them with reliable sources of information.

A Summary of the Shelley Legend

"The Shelley Legend," we are told by Professor Smith[3] (p. iii), "is a term used to characterize fallacious views about the life of Shelley and his writings which have grown up principally under the careful supervision first of Mary Shelley and after her death, in 1851, of Lady Shelley, wife of the poet's son, Sir Percy Florence Shelley. It includes also various other chicaneries subsequently foisted by others upon admirers of the poet and his writings." So numerous are these "fal-

[3] From this point on I shall, for the sake of convenience, refer only to Professor Smith as the author of *The Shelley Legend*. Though at least half the book was not originally written by Professor Smith, he directed the whole project and obviously edited and approved all materials printed.

lacious views" that, as we have seen, "at least fifty per cent of the present attitude toward Shelley still stems from this [Lady Shelley's] cult" (p. 305). In other words, the real Shelley has been so thoroughly obscured that he is not to be discovered in any of the many biographies; Shelley has become a legendary character.

The legend was built by Mary Shelley and Lady Jane Shelley. The definition above fails to specify Forgeries separately as a third factor because it is included in the general charge against Mary and Lady Shelley.

The method used by Professor Smith to prove the existence of the Shelley Legend is to present the following:

I. A review of Mary Shelley's life with special reference to her activities in connection with Shelley biography. She is accused of assisting Medwin with his (extremely inaccurate) biographical sketch of Shelley in his *Conversations of Lord Byron*, 1824, of spreading false information about Harriet through Hunt and Medwin, of withholding information about Shelley during her lifetime or preventing such information from being published; and finally of creating the Shelley Legend by presenting him to the public as an angelic character in her 1839 edition of his *Poetical Works* and her 1840 edition of his Prose Works (*Essays, Letters from Abroad*, &c.). In the latter she was "most selective and most discreet" (p. 28); she also altered the *Six Weeks' Tour* and the letters she printed.

II. A review of Lady Jane Shelley's activities in collecting, arranging, and printing privately materials concerning Shelley, and of her efforts to get written a suitable biography of Shelley. She is directly charged (1) with having withheld from Dowden documents which she did not wish to be seen; (2) with having permitted Dowden only a fleeting glimpse of the original MSS; (3) with forcing Dowden to express her opinions ("almost by dictation," p. iii) instead of his own;

and (4) with having failed to print in *Shelley and Mary* true copies of Shelley and Mary's Journal and of the letters, and of having deliberately omitted or altered significant passages.

III. An account of the history of Shelley forgeries, especially of the activities of the master forger, Major George Byron. The main purpose of this account is to show: (a) that many forgeries came into the possession of the Shelley family and have both unintentionally and purposely been used as genuine documents, and (b) to create a general impression that no document relating to Shelley can be trusted until a handwriting expert has pronounced it genuine or its provenance has been established by incontrovertible proof.

IV. An attempt to prove, and thus fully to establish the purpose of III, that five Shelley and Mary letters and one MS, all heretofore (with one exception) unsuspected as forgeries, are forgeries. Four of these contain evidence that Shelley thought (or at least said) that Harriet had been morally lax in conduct. It is therefore the contention of the author that with their removal as evidence the charge against Harriet collapses.

V. The author throughout the book implies that Mary Shelley and Lady Shelley were guilty of conniving with a forger to manufacture false documents.

VI. Interspersed passages relating to Claire Clairmont, which have for their purpose the establishment of the opinions (a) that Claire and Shelley were lovers, "physically and spiritually," (b) that the Hoppner story is true, and (c) that because of Mary's and Lady Shelley's dislike for Claire they are responsible for her consistent mistreatment by biographers.

The result of all this is the revelation of the real Shelley, already described, and the contention that the whole documentary foundation of Shelley biography is unsound.

An Examination of the Shelley Legend

I propose to take up each of the above points in turn. First, however, it should be clearly understood that Professor Smith has found no new sources of information, and that with the exception of his claims about newly-discovered forgeries, he is using materials which have been used repeatedly by Shelley scholars. If, therefore, Professor Smith has presented anything different from the best documented biographies and biographical studies, it is either because (1) he has given a different interpretation to the evidence, or (2) has misinterpreted the evidence.

I. *The Charge Against Mary Shelley.*

Professor Smith finds it difficult to substantiate his charge against Mary Shelley. No one has ever disputed or been deceived by the fact that she created an idealistic portrait of Shelley, such as any idolizing wife might have done, in her prefaces and notes to the *Posthumous Poems* (1824), *Poetical Works* (1839), and *Essays*, &c. (1840). There is, and can be, no charge that she published falsehoods.

Until 1839 Mary was restrained by Sir Timothy Shelley from bringing Shelley's name before the public. Had she done so, her slender income, on which the welfare of her son depended, would have been cut off. The *Posthumous Poems* (1824) would have been followed by a volume of Shelley's Prose, if the former had not been withdrawn from sale on the demand of Sir Timothy. In fact, it is clear that had Mary been permitted to do so, she would have given the public, long before 1839, both Shelley's poetical and prose works and a Life of Shelley.

But the biography that Mary would have written would have been governed by a principle which she followed con-

sistently all her life—that of sparing the living from unnecessary pain. She would have played down her own part in
Shelley's life, for she disliked publicity. But that was second-
ary. Her chief regard was for the welfare of Ianthe Shelley
and Claire Clairmont. The life that she would have written
would have given no more about the separation than the bare
fact that it did occur; and it would have omitted Claire
entirely, not because of her relationship with Shelley, but because of her connection with Lord Byron. It is perfectly true
and altogether honorable that she should have used all her
influence to keep these matters from discussion by the public.
Claire had to earn her living as a governess, and respectable
employers would not have entrusted their children to a
woman whose reputation was the subject of public scandal.

It still remains, however, to see what Mary actually did to
control Shelley biography, As an introduction to the *Posthumous Poems* she requested Leigh Hunt (at that time in
Italy) to write an essay on Shelley. Hunt wrote it but, despite
Mary's repeated requests, did not finish it in time for inclu-
sion in the *Posthumous Poems*. In 1825 he sent it to the *West-
minster Review*, and the editor, Sir John Bowring, sent it to
Peacock and Mary for appraisal. Peacock objected to its publication, both on the grounds of inaccuracies concerning Harriet, and of its causing trouble with Sir Timothy Shelley, with
whom he had (for Mary) just concluded arrangements inci-
dent to the publication and suppression of the *Posthumous
Poems*. Mary wrote to Hunt on April 8, 1825, pointing out
two errors of fact, one being that "Shelley did not allow
Harriet half his income—she received £200 a year. Mr. Westbrook had always made his daughter an allowance even while
she lived with Shelley—which of course was continued to her
after their separation." She also requested Hunt "to omit all
allusion to Claire. After the death of L. B[yron] in the thick
of memoirs, scandals, and turning up old stories she has never

been alluded to . . . In fact poor Claire has been buried in entire oblivion and to bring her from this even for the sake of defending her would I am sure pain her greatly and do her mischief. . . . Allegra no more—she at present absent and forgotten—on Sir Tim's death she will come in for a legacy which may enable her to enter into society, perhaps to marry, if she wishes it—if the past be not [? revived]."[4] On December 28, 1825, she pointed out further an error "which is vital. It regards Shelley & Harriet—where you found your reasoning on a mistake as to fact—they did not part by mutual consent—and Shelley's justification, to me obvious, rests on other grounds."[5]

When Hunt published the article in his *Lord Byron and Some of His Contemporaries* (1828), he retained the "mutual consent" statement, but omitted any mention of Claire.

Three conclusions from this affair are inescapable: (1) Mary wished to have Hunt's article published; (2) she had nothing to do with its composition except to point out errors of fact, and to request the removal of Claire's name; and (3) she tried to correct errors concerning Harriet.

In spite of these facts, however, in commenting upon Charles Brown's letter of 1825, in which the charges against Harriet are repeated, Professor Smith says (p. 27): "Brown . . . merely phrases more emphatically what Medwin and Hunt were to repeat and what thenceforth through the efforts of Mary and the machinations of Lady Shelley was to become the nucleus of the Shelley legend." And yet Professor Smith never presents any evidence to show that Mary at any time did anything to establish false facts about Harriet.

He does, however, make one attempt to lend support to his statement. "Mary," he says (p. 26), "did not, however, dare to antagonize Medwin; she gave him aid apparently on

---

[4] *Letters of Mary W. Shelley*, I, 317.
[5] *Ibid.*, I, 339-340.

the Shelley parts of his Byron book [*Conversations of Lord Byron*, 1824], and drew thereby a sharp rebuke from Trelawny." Trelawny's letter thus referred to had no reference to Medwin's book. The following passage in his letter of October 20, 1829, refers only to Thomas Moore and his *Life of Byron:* ". . . had Shelley's *detractor* and your very good *friend* Tom Moore—made the request, I feel confident he would not have been so fobbed off—as is proved by your having aided him in Byron's memoirs."[6] "Shelley's detractor" and Mary's "very good friend Tom Moore" are one and the same person. The next paragraph of Trelawny's letter introduces a long tale about Medwin's villanies in connection with his wife, whose fortune of £10,000 Medwin had run through. He taunts Mary by saying, "You used to like and laud him [Medwin] and thought me rash and violent in asserting him to be a coward, a liar, and a scoundrel—nevertheless he has proved himself all these."[6a]

Mary's reply to this is: "Did I uphold and dared [*sic*] Medwin—I thought that I had always disliked him—I am sure I thought him a great annoyance . . . He was Jane's friend more than any ones—to be sure, we did not desire a duel nor an horsewhipping—and Lord Byron and Mrs. Beauclerk worked hard to promote peace—Can anything be as frightful as the account you give? Poor Mrs. Medwin."[7]

Moreover, on this matter we have Mary's definite word. On October 10 [1824] she wrote to Mrs. Hunt:

Have you heard of Medwin's book—notes on conversations that he had at Pisa with L[ord] B[yron] (when tipsy) every one is to be in it every one will be angry. He wanted me to have a hand in it but I declined—years ago "When a man died the worms ate

---

[6] R. Glynn Grylls, *Mary Shelley* (London: Oxford University Press, 1938), p. 217.

[6a] *Ibid.*, p. 218 and note 2 on p. 217.

[7] *Letters of Mary W. Shelley*, II, 24.

him"—now a new set of worms feed on the carcase of the scandal
that he leaves behind him and grow fat upon the world's love of
tittle tattle—I will not be numbered among them.[8]

Professor Smith's statement is therefore absolutely false.
He makes it because he wishes to find somewhere evidence
that Mary sanctioned the "parted by mutual consent" story.
Medwin said nothing about "mutual consent" in his horribly
inaccurate sketch of Shelley's life in the *Conversations;* he
made it in his memoir of Shelley in the *Athenaeum* for 1832,
having taken it from Hunt's *Lord Byron,* &c. of 1828. Professor Smith is not merely snatching at straws; he is making
straws.

Mary's refusal to assist Trelawny with a life of Shelley
is too well known to require discussion. Professor Smith can
find nothing helpful in it. He must also be disappointed with
her willingness to assist with the Galignani edition of Shelley's
Poetical Works in 1829, and with the non-acceptance of her
offer to write a sketch of Shelley's life, the "chief merit" of
which would be "the absence of incorrectness." On Hogg's
"Shelley at Oxford" articles in the *New Monthly Magazine*
(1832) Mary, of course, had no influence whatsoever.

This is the sum and substance of Mary's progress toward
creating a Shelley legend up to 1839. Hunt, Medwin, and
Cyrus Redding (Galignani edition) had indeed made something of a legend through their inaccuracies, but it was
entirely without the connivance of Mary Shelley, who had
protested to Trelawny the "slurring over the real truth" in
Hunt's account.

After this much ado about nothing we are informed sud-
denly (p. 28) that "Mary Creates the Shelley Legend." One
might expect something solid here, but after a fourteen-line

[8] *Ibid.,* I, 308; see also a similar statement on I, 315, and J. C. Hobhouse's letter of November 12, 1824, to Mary (*Shelley and Mary,* IV,
1188-89).

quotation from Mary and twenty-five lines of explanation, the act of creation is over. The creation is in two parts. First, Mary's edition of Shelley's *Poetical Works*, 1839, "with explanatory notes," which afforded her an opportunity "at least to place her ideal Shelley before the world." It is admitted that she introduced "into the notes as much biographical matter as she dared," but presumably it is a fault that Shelley appears "in the glowing light supplied by her noble and generous art of praising." What damning evidence Professor Smith finds in the fourteen-line quotation from the first paragraph of Mary's Preface, he does not tell us. How is it possible to tell the world more emphatically that the facts of Shelley's private life have not yet been told, that they have been withheld because they affect others, that she does not wish them related until they can be given without "any colouring of the truth," and that she is perfectly aware that Shelley's life contained "errors of action." They are bold and noble words and are worth repeating:

I abstain from any remark on the occurrences of his private life; except, inasmuch as the passions which they engendered, inspired his poetry. This is not the time to relate the truth; and I should reject any colouring of the truth. No account of these events has ever been given at all approaching reality in their details, either as regards himself or others.

The second part of Mary's act of creation was the publication in 1840 of her edition of Shelley's unpublished prose, entitled *Essays, Letters from Abroad*, &c. Professor Smith's criticisms of this work are slender and distressingly inaccurate. First, it is objected that Mary "was most selective and most discreet." He does not note Mary's frank statement in the Preface: "This concludes the essays and fragments of Shelley. I do not give them as the whole that he left, but as the most interesting portion. A Treatise on Political Reform and other fragments remain, to be published when his works assume a complete shape." Very little of importance has been published since except "A Philosophical View of Reform," the "Essay on Christianity," and the treatise "On Devils."

Professor Smith's next objection is singular indeed in that it apparently reveals his ignorance of the fact that Mary's *History of a Six Weeks' Tour* was originally published in 1817. In the *Essays*, &c. Mary reprinted the *History* exactly as it was published earlier, except for a few verbal changes which consist mainly of corrections in spelling and substitutions of better synonyms, such as "driver" for "conductor."[8a] It is certainly unreasonable to censure Mary for not publishing the Journal in its original state. Professor Smith's mistaken charge is that: "She suppressed passages and names in the *History of a Six Weeks' Tour*. Claire, when permitted to appear at all, was reduced to 'C***,' and the whole account was altered so as to give the impression that the tour was an unclouded and lovely romance amid the grandeurs of nature, and that all was one sweet and prolonged harmony of song. How different was the reality: the sick mule, Shelley's sprained ankle, the dirt and horrors amid the wolfish creatures who kept the inns where they stayed . . . a veritable tragicomedy of errors." Whatever changes were made from the original journal were made by Mary in 1817, long before it could have occurred to her to create a Shelley legend. Moreover, this looks more like a determination to find fault than to state the truth, for the original journal proves that the tour was a happy one. It may have been a comedy of errors, but not a tragi-comedy. Furthermore, the items enumerated after "How different was the reality" are all in the printed *Tour*, except the "sick mule," which does not exist even in

[8a] The few differences between the 1817 and 1840 editions are recorded by Ingpen in the Julian Edition, VI, 356-358.

the original journal. I suppose Professor Smith has confused the small ass with which the Shelleys set out from Paris and which proved too weak even to carry their baggage, with the mule which they purchased to replace the ass. Neither the ass nor the mule was "sick." If Professor Smith is distressed over Mary's suppression of "the dirt and horrors," etc., this passage from the *Tour* (1840 edition) ought to be helpful: "As we prepared our dinner in a place so filthy, that the sight of it alone was sufficient to destroy our appetite, the people of the village collected around us, squalid with dirt, their countenances expressing everything that is disgusting and brutal."

Professor Smith's third charge against Mary's edition of the *Essays* is (p. 29) that she "altered Shelley's letters . . . with numerous editings, changes, and suppressions, so that by 1850 and 1852 when the poetry and prose volumes were again issued by Edward Moxon, the Shelley legend was well on its way to establishment." One grows impatient with Professor Smith at times because he fails to offer any evidence to support his sweeping statements. In this case all he could have shown was Mary's occasional substitution of a dash or initial for the name, such as C—for Claire, and her complete omission of all references to Claire and Byron's affair. In doing this, Mary was following a practice which she had believed correct since she had requested Hunt in 1825 to omit any reference to Claire. Mary's desire to publish the letters as fully as circumstances permitted is illustrated by a note not made by Professor Smith. In 1839 she had requested Hunt's permission to use for the *Essays* the Shelley letters he had printed in his *Lord Byron and Some of His Contemporaries* in 1828. On November 14, 1839, she wrote to Hunt: "I see a few asterisks & omissions in the letters of Shelley you published—were these wholly private & indifferent or did some temporary or modest personal reason cause them—If the latter pray let me replace them—let me have the originals for a few days."[9] Hunt did lend the original letters, and Mary printed more complete and accurate texts.[9a]

Finally, it may be recalled that on p. 27 Professor Smith calls the charges against Harriet "the nucleus of the Shelley legend." It is odd indeed that Mary created the Shelley legend without the slightest reference to this nucleus.

And thus Mary Shelley created the Shelley legend. Subsequent biographers have been so hypnotized by her brief prefaces and notes, in spite of her warning that the truth as to Shelley's private life had not yet been told, that they, according to Professor Smith, have been unable to exercise independent judgment upon the facts which have become available in great quantities. Her unsuccessful struggle to prevent the publication of Medwin's *Life of Shelley* (1847) is very naturally viewed by Professor Smith as an effort to prevent her ideal Shelley from being shattered. He will not, of course, allow the force of her statement to Medwin (p. 29) that Ianthe, Shelley's daughter, "who is innocent of all blame," might be injured by the publication. To her reasons for desiring Medwin's *Life* not to be published Mary could have added her conviction that Medwin was incapable of writing anything accurately. And it is a fact that Medwin's *Life* is the most incorrect biography of Shelley, and possibly of anyone, in existence.

It is my conviction that the charge made by Professor Smith against Mary Shelley is not true.

II. *The Charge Against Lady Shelley.*

The charge against Mary Shelley is silly and cannot be sustained by any evidence. The charge against Lady Shelley,

---

[9] *Letters of Mary W. Shelley*, II, 141.

[9a] H. B. Forman collated the texts by Hunt and Mary and recorded the variants. See the footnotes to his *Prose Works of Shelley* (1880), I, 128, 150-151, etc.

however, is very serious, for it strikes at the very foundation of Shelley scholarship. The charge is not true, and I shall prove that Professor Smith, in making it, has not reported faithfully on a relatively simple body of materials.[10]

In 1886 Edward Dowden published the first fully docu-

---

[10] I pass over as irrelevant Professor Smith's account of Lady Shelley's Shelley shrines, her employment and subsequent dismissal of Hogg as the official biographer, her *Shelley Memorials* (1859), her conflict with Peacock and with Trelawny, and her numerous other activities. These have no bearing whatsoever on the charge that she actually established a Shelley legend. It is admitted that she had no influence whatever on Hogg, who had, according to his own published statement, not only access to all the original MSS belonging to Lady Shelley but actual possession of them ("every scrap," he says). That Lady Shelley should dismiss him as a biographer and should repossess the MSS upon the discovery that he had altered and falsified documents was entirely proper, and is in itself proof that she was concerned about the truth. Hogg had done much more even than Lady Shelley knew, for not until recently has it been known fully how radically he changed letters in his own possession and never seen by Lady Shelley. Her opposition to Peacock's story that Shelley was content with Harriet until he met Mary was also in the main right. Peacock's error on this point has been established by overwhelming proof. It must have been Lady Shelley's strong conviction of Peacock's better knowledge of the real truth that led her to espouse the baseless theory that Peacock was himself the guilty man, that on the October 1813 trip to Edinburgh with Shelley and Harriet he had made successful advances to Harriet. It is a fable that Peacock is one of the most reliable witnesses on Shelley biography. He stands convicted of having committed a number of very serious blunders. For example, his contention that Shelley protested word by word the changes required by Ollier in *Laon and Cythna* is absolutely false and has led to a misrepresentation of Shelley's attitude toward that work and the public almost to this day. (See Marcel Kessel, *Times Literary Supplement*, Sept., 1933, p. 592, and F. L. Jones, "The Revision of *Laon and Cythna*," *JEGP*, XXXII (July 1933), 366-372.) As for Lady Shelley's *Shelley Memorials* (1859), though a valuable book when published, it has been known by every intelligent scholar as a family portrait of Shelley and has been used by them only as a source book for materials not available elsewhere.

There is no need to notice Kegan Paul's life of *William Godwin* or Mrs. Julian Marshall's *Life and Letters of Mary Shelley*. They are useful books even to this day, not for their opinions, but for the documents of which they mainly consist.

mented *Life of Shelley* in two large volumes. Dowden had
access to a tremendous quantity of materials, a considerable
portion of which were in Lady Shelley's hands. Upon
Dowden's book is based the greater part of subsequent Shelley
research, though the publication of Ingpen's *Letters of Shelley*
(1909, &c.) and *Shelley in England* (1917) and of other
important books and articles have contributed much additional
information. Professor Newman I. White's recent *Shelley*
(1940) is more heavily documented than Dowden's *Life*, and
incorporating all Shelley scholarship since Dowden, has
greatly relaxed the scholar's dependence upon Dowden. If it
can be shown, however, as Professor Smith attempts to do, that
Dowden's *Life* is unreliable factually, then White's great
biography (in that it utilizes substantially the same source
materials) is also to a considerable extent discredited, and
present Shelley scholarship is a travesty of errors.

So important is Professor Smith's account of Dowden's
relationship with Lady Shelley that the main portion of it
(pp. 258-260) must be given here (italics are my own):

Edward Dowden was chosen to prepare the official life based
upon the family archives, because Dr. Garnett, who had cham-
pioned the Shelley Legend against Peacock and all others and
whom the family would have chosen to write the biography, was
too much engrossed with his work at the British Museum.
Dowden's task, begun in 1883, shortly after the Shelleys had
privately printed and then suppressed their version of the journals
of *Shelley and Mary*, was the three-year toiling of a conscientious
but baffled and troubled spirit. *Had he been given free access to all
the manuscripts, letters, and other sources in the Shelley family's
possession* and let alone to write according to his own judgment,
his biography might not have received the slating it so justly merited
from Matthew Arnold and Mark Twain.

. . . Though he was able to appreciate Shelley's great poetic
gifts, he could view his conduct only with an uneasy conscience
which, combined with the promptings of Sir Percy and Lady

Shelley, caused him to indulge in constant apology, wire-drawn explanation, and perfumed and labored circumlocution. The Shelley family did not wish Shelley, his second wife Mary, or William Godwin to receive any adverse judgment, and any of the glaring departures from Victorian standards they wished suppressed, toned down, explained away, glossed over, or apologized for. *There developed, then, as would be expected, a very definite conflict. Dowden, on the one hand, doing his best to extract from the family the facts contained in letters and journals and to maintain an independence of judgment, and Lady Shelley as strenuously resisting in giving him access to basic materials, except now and then piecemeal.* In other words, she expected Dowden to do the impossible. He was, furthermore, *obliged to use the printed version of* Shelley and Mary; *only for a brief moment did he once have the precious original diaries in his hands, and then he found, to his great discomfiture, that the printed version was a bowdlerized account differing throughout from the manuscript text.*

His first task should have been to insist on the use of the manuscript text of the journals, but *since Lady Shelley had already prepared her own printed version of them, Dowden was compelled to make his notes and annotations in that.* Not until someone has collated and corrected Lady Shelley's *Shelley and Mary* with the original manuscript journals will Shelley biography be on a sound basis. *Dowden's account, therefore, was bound to reflect what Lady Shelley wished the official life to reflect. She was, too, very chary about letting him use the contents of her archives. In a letter to Garnett in 1885, after he had gathered materials far and wide for two years, he complained that the family had shown him very little. . . .*

It is reported that more than once, because of family interference, Dowden was tempted to abandon the whole project:

"They are very kind at Boscombe, but I feel oppressed by the duty of considering all Lady Shelley's tender enthusiasms."

He apparently wrote along freely enough until he came to the chapters which dealt with the separation of Shelley from Harriet; then he met from Sir Percy and Lady Shelley the same sort of difficulties that Hogg and Peacock had endured.

In a letter to Garnett dated May 15, 1885, Dowden writes he has followed Garnett's views; but he added:

". . . no charge of grave misconduct against Harriet before the separation has ever been brought except by an unknown person communicating with Godwin after her death."

He wished to clear Harriet of imaginary accusations and to do her justice, for he found "people here and there thinking there must be good evidence that she sinned grievously." He added that he was prepared to modify his views if Sir Percy and Lady Shelley could "indicate facts or interpret known facts in a way which shall show things in a different light." He was distressed when they made known their disapproval of his account as much too favorable to Harriet, and they appealed to Dr. Garnett as mediator and referee.

When Dowden was called to Boscombe, therefore, he encountered a barrage from Lady Shelley against Harriet. Lady Shelley, he wrote Garnett, had "filled up all the gaps with conjectures which time seemed to have altered into something like certainties— 'Harriet was weakly during pregnancy—Eliza pressed her to drink wine etc. etc.—Shelley never loved Harriet etc.' " He pointed out to Garnett that he could not include such charges without evidence, nor was he convinced at this time of infidelity on Harriet's part. *He complained that the family had shown him "unhappily very little," three or four short letters of Shelley to his father, another to Charles Grove, and the letter of Harriet to Hookham.*

The source of Professor Smith's information is principally *Letters About Shelley,* ed. by R. S. Garnett (1917), pp. 77-151; additional facts are drawn from *Letters of Edward Dowden and His Correspondents* (1914), and *Fragments from Old Letters, E. D. to E. D. W.* (1914). In the passage quoted at length above, three important points are made by Professor Smith. These I shall examine in the light of Professor Smith's own sources of information.

(1) *That Lady Shelley withheld from Dowden documents which she did not wish to be seen.* This charge is repeated

endlessly. It is based on a passage which Professor Smith refers to on p. 258 and again on 259, as follows: "She was, too, very chary about letting him use the contents of her archives. In a letter to Garnett in 1885 . . . he complained that the family had shown him very little" (p. 258);—"He pointed out to Garnett that he could not include such charges without evidence, nor was he convinced at this time of infidelity on Harriet's part. He complained that the family had shown him 'unhappily very little,' three or four short letters of Shelley to his father, another to Charles Grove, and the letter of Harriet to Hookham" (p. 259).

This is what Dowden actually wrote to Garnett on May 17, 1885: "Up to the point at which my work has been seen by them [the separation story, 1814] they [the Shelleys] had unhappily very little to show me—indeed nothing except three or four short letters of Shelley to his father, one to Charles Grove from York, and the letter of Harriet to Hookham. Which fact however does not lessen my sense of their great kindness and perfect courtesy."[11] This cannot possibly mean that the Shelleys refused to place documents at Dowden's disposal; it means precisely what Dowden intended to say, that the Shelleys "had unhappily very little to show me" concerning Shelley's life before July 1814. How could the Shelleys have these documents? They were, very naturally, in the hands of Harriet's family (the Esdailes and Westbrooks), of Sir Timothy's son John Shelley and his lawyer Whitton, of Hogg and Peacock, of Miss Hitchener's descendants—and from none of these could the Shelleys have procured them.

We have Dowden's own word on this matter, in the second paragraph of the Preface to his *Life*. He says: "My first thanks are due to Sir Percy and Lady Shelley. I have had access to all the Shelley papers in their possession, and per-

---

[11] *Letters About Shelley*, p. 118.

mission to make use of them without reserve." It should also be noted that in his enumeration of the general contents of the Boscombe papers Dowden mentions several documents which are not printed in *Shelley and Mary:* "Mary Shelley's transcript of the journal of Edward Williams, some unpublished writings of Shelley, and legal papers." There are also numerous other facts which show clearly that Dowden saw the original MSS; some of these will appear in other parts of this paper. If Professor Smith's charge is true, then Edward Dowden is guilty of a flagrant violation of truth.[12]

(2) *That Lady Shelley permitted Dowden only a fleeting glimpse of the original MSS.* Professor Smith's words are (and incessantly he repeats the charge): "He [Dowden] was, furthermore, obliged to use the printed version of *Shelley and Mary;* only for a brief moment did he once have the precious original diaries in his hands, and then he found, to his great discomfiture, that the printed version was a bowdlerized account differing throughout from the manuscript text" (p. 258). Speaking mildly, this statement is extremely inaccurate. "Obliged," "only for a brief moment," "diaries," "bowdlerized," "differing throughout"—where are these to be found in Dowden's letter on which this statement is based—his letter to Richard Garnett dated December 28,

---

[12] Professor Smith's perversion of the truth is further illustrated by this statement on p. 116: "We can now see clearly why Dowden kept bitterly complaining to Garnett about his having to use 'abstracts of abstracts' rather than the originals, few of which apparently Lady Shelley ever allowed him to examine." On December 6, 1883, Dowden wrote to Garnett: "It has grieved me to hear that Lady Shelley has not been well. Her last letter (sending your 'abstracts of abstracts' of Miss Clairmont's and Mrs. Godwin's letters with comments on them—spoke with warm gratitude of what you had done for Shelley's sake and for theirs" (*Letters About Shelley,* p. 85). Claire had made abstracts of Mrs. Godwin's letters; Garnett had made abstracts of Claire's abstracts; hence the "abstracts of abstracts." Dowden not only saw Claire's original abstracts later, but he printed them in Appendix B of his *Life* (II, 541-551).

1885, after a visit to Boscombe in the early autumn: "I made the alarming discovery that 'Shelley and Mary,' wherever I looked, is a far from accurate rendering of the MSS and that a careful collation will be necessary."[13]

It is clear from this sentence that Dowden was doing exactly what any careful scholar would do—checking the printed transcripts (not only of the diaries, but of the letters) with the original MSS. It is equally clear that this was only a preliminary testing ("wherever I looked," not "throughout"), and that he was troubled about inaccuracies, not deliberate changes and significant omissions. It is also clear that Dowden had no notion there would be any difficulty in getting access to the MSS when he was ready to make the collation.

Professor Smith also makes nothing of Dowden's determination to make "a careful collation" with the original MSS. Much more significant is his failure to tell us the very evident fact that *Dowden did make the collation*. Dowden's statement in his Preface is strictly true: that he had "access to all the Shelley papers" and that he had "permission *to use them without reserve*."

To make the story clear, it is necessary to review the facts. Upon being invited to write a life of Shelley, Dowden visited the Shelleys at Boscombe Manor, Bournemouth. He was given a copy of *Shelley and Mary*, which, according to Sir Percy Florence Shelley's preliminary note, had "been prepared for the press by Lady Shelley, with the object of preserving from destruction the precious records in her possession. They comprise all the letters and other documents of a biographical character at present [1882] in the hands of Shelley's representatives." Dowden took the volumes home with him to Dublin and began working. Though *Shelley and Mary* was invaluable and furnished the backbone of his *Life*, it was by no means sufficient for a full rendering of Shelley's life. For one thing, it gave no material whatsoever for

[13] *Letters About Shelley*, p. 145.

Shelley's life before his elopement with Mary Godwin on July 28, 1814. Dowden worked for two years and collected an immense amount of material in addition to that in *Shelley and Mary*, as his letters and Preface to the *Life of Shelley* very clearly show.

By that time he had written a good deal, and decided that a trip to Boscombe Manor was necessary in order to effect possible further gatherings of material, and in order to check on the reliability of the *Shelley and Mary* transcripts. As we have seen, he did check the transcripts sufficiently to convince himself that it would be necessary to collate everything he had used or would use in his *Life* with the original MSS. On this visit he had time for only "one night" at Boscombe. He probably never had any intention of collating the whole 1243 pages of *Shelley and Mary* with the MSS, but only those documents (numerous indeed) which he meant to use. Since the Journal was the backbone of his narrative, it can be assumed without hestitation that he collated it from beginning to end, that is, to the end of Shelley's life. It would not be necessary by any means to collate all the letters, though virtually all of Shelley's and many of Mary's letters would have to be collated.

Dowden's willingness to delay the collating until the biography was near completion is in itself a convincing argument that, though the inaccuracies of *Shelley and Mary* were "alarming," they were far from being vital or serious. If he had thought them vital, he would not have proceeded with the *Life* until the whole of *Shelley and Mary* had been collated, for he would then have run the risk of having to rewrite his entire book. No scholar would take such a risk.

I repeat that Dowden did actually make the collation. It was in the early autumn of 1885 that he had made his "alarming discovery" at Boscombe and had decided that "a careful collation will be necessary." Since then he had made rapid progress. On April 30, 1886, he wrote to E. D. W[est]: "I want if possible to postpone my visit to the Shelleys till mid-summer; I have much collation to do and I want to do it all at a single visit. They are very kind at Boscombe, but I feel oppressed by the duty of considering all Lady Shelley's tender enthusiasm."[14] On May 14, 1886, he wrote to the same correspondent: "I decided to postpone my work on the Shelley MSS. [Lady Shelley's] until the summer vacation; and, meanwhile, it will be my endeavour to fall tooth and nail on what I can do without the said MSS., and by very close application, try to be well advanced with my work by July."[15] On June 25, 1886, he wrote again to E.D.W.: "I am divided between the wish to go off at once now to Boscombe, and the doubt whether I ought not to stay until the Dublin elections are over. It is a time when a couple of votes ought not to be thrown away; on the other hand it is very desirable that I should have made my last gathering of material and should be at my desk, where alone I can make progress. I shall make my stay at Boscombe as short as possible."[16]

Dowden finally made his long-projected visit in August 1886, and it can be assumed that while there he did precisely what he went there to do—collated a considerable part of *Shelley and Mary* with the original MSS. Only one of his letters from Boscombe (to his brother, Bishop J. Dowden) has been printed, and this,[17] though it says nothing about collating MSS, expresses great satisfaction with his visit.[17a]

I think that the above facts, coupled with Dowden's own

[14] *Fragments from Old Letters, E.D. to E.D.W.*, p. 179. Professor Smith prints only the last sentence!

[15] *Ibid.*, p. 181.

[16] *Ibid.*, p. 182.

[17] *Letters of Edward Dowden and His Correspondents*, p. 221.

[17a] Dowden's *Life* gives frequent evidence of his use of Lady Shelley's original MSS. Specific uses of the MS Journal are to be found on I, 457, 480, 505. Other examples are at I, 493, where Dowden prints a letter from the MS and restores omissions in the *Shelley and Mary* text; and at II, 21, 46, 47, 67-68, 325, where Dowden prints (from Lady Shelley's papers) letters and a MS which are not in *Shelley and Mary*.

positive words in his Preface ("all the Shelley papers," "without reserve") prove as completely false Professor Smith's charge that Dowden was restrained from using the original MSS except on one brief occasion. Dowden could have used the MSS as often as he chose to go to Boscombe Manor.

(3) *That Lady Shelley ("almost by dictation") forced Dowden to express her opinions instead of his own.*

This accusation is as false as the two which have just been examined, as anyone can prove for himself by reading pp. 113-134 of *Letters About Shelley*.

The only objections the Shelleys ever raised were with reference to one chapter; and here their objections were only two: (1) the treatment of the separation, and (2) satirical epithets applied to Godwin. Dowden wrote to Garnett on May 15, 1885: "I fear I must soon run over to London for a day or two to confer with Sir Percy and Lady Shelley. Two things seem to be unsatisfactory to them. First my treatment of the separation from Harriet. . . . I have also pained them by certain half-satirical references to Godwin as the 'Sage' and the 'philosopher.' "[18] Garnett wrote Dowden on the same day, May 15: "I saw Sir Percy and Lady Shelley yesterday. They are evidently not quite satisfied with your chapter on the separation between Shelley and Harriet . . . They express themselves highly gratified with all the rest of the book."[19]

In order to spare Dowden a trip to London to confer with the Shelleys, Garnett, supporting Dowden entirely, undertook to talk with Sir Percy and Lady Shelley. He assured Dowden: "I would not allege anything against her [Harriet] which could not be proved by unimpeachable testimony."[20]

Still not knowing how serious the discussion with the

[18] *Letters About Shelley*, pp. 113-114.
[19] *Ibid.*, p. 115.
[20] *Ibid.*, p. 115.

Shelleys might be, Dowden wrote on May 17, asserting his determination from the start to deal independently with the evidence:

Long since, I said in a letter to Sir Percy and Lady Shelley that I wrote on the understanding that their responsibility was limited to the choice of a competent biographer and to his using documents with fidelity; but I understand how they must feel a special concern about this portion of the story. . . .

The difficulty I anticipated from the first arose from my perceiving that Lady Shelley (guided by the best of feelings) had filled up all the gaps with conjectures which time seemed to have altered into something like certainties—"Harriet was weakly during pregnancy—Eliza pressed her to drink wine etc. etc.—Shelley never loved Harriet etc."[21] . . .

To close my long letter I may say for your own judicious hearing that I fancy Sir Percy in the kindest way imagines it will be an advantage to me that my book should receive a sort of imprimatur from the representatives of Shelley. But, as a fact, I should like nothing worse than that it should be supposed that I had in the slightest degree forfeited my independence. So that it would be in some respects an advantage if I could say in my preface that Sir Percy and Lady Shelley, although their views and mine did not always coincide, had placed the documents they possess at my disposal.[22]

[21] Note the perversion of Professor Smith's account at this point. "When," he writes, "Dowden was called to Boscombe, therefore, he encountered a barrage from Lady Shelley against Harriet. Lady Shelley, he wrote Garnett, had 'filled up all the gaps . . .' " Dowden was not *called*; nor was he at any time a man whom the Shelleys could call. He himself thought of going to London to see the Shelleys, but, as we have seen, he did not go. He therefore did not encounter a "barrage from Lady Shelley." His quotations of Lady Shelley's speeches about Harriet refer to his first visit to Boscombe in July 1883, and these, as he says, led him "from the first" to anticipate difficulty on this part of Shelley's life.

[22] *Letters About Shelley*, pp. 116, 118.

Garnett replied, "I am with you in all essential points,"[23] and on June 5 wrote:

I have had a very satisfactory interview with Sir Percy and Lady Shelley today. I had feared that they would wish you to espouse a theory of Sir Percy's, which connects the separation with the second visit to Edinburgh,[24] and also that they would have had you bear hardly upon Harriet. With this anticipation I had prepared a memorandum, which I enclose solely for yourself, that you may see how I should have treated these matters. But they readily acquiesced in my view [which completely supported Dowden], and it was not necessary to produce the memorandum at all. They are pleased with your deferring to Sir Percy's opinion as concerns Godwin [the satirical epithets] . . . I do not know of anything that could lead to further discussion if you can see your way to a few merely verbal alterations."[25]

Garnett returned to Sir Percy the MS of Dowden's Chapter VII with some memoranda, and Sir Percy forwarded the MS to Dowden with the memoranda, the same being received by Dowden by July 9.

There was no further discussion with the Shelleys about Chapter VII or about anything else. When Dowden made his final visit to Boscombe in August 1886, he carried the revised chapter with him. He reports to his brother on August 9: "My crucial chapter, which I read for you, has given entire satisfaction to Sir P. and Lady Shelley. This,

[23] *Ibid.*, p. 119.

[24] Lady Shelley, though yielding to Dowden and Garnett, did not change her mind about Peacock being responsible for the separation and about Harriet's infidelity before the separation. In all the copies of *Shelley and Mary* still in her possession she wrote out her reasons for holding such an opinion. The signed entry is dated December 21, 1885, and is printed in Grylls, *Mary Shelley* (1938), pp. 269-271.

[25] *Letters About Shelley*, p. 124.

although it was more like a judge's charge than an advocate's speech. And I am pleasantly surprised."[26]

The truth then is that instead of taking his opinions "almost by dictation" from the Shelleys, Dowden was seriously questioned by them on only one point, on which he did not yield an inch. The theory which the Shelleys still devoutly believed, he would not even mention in his book.

Professor Smith's charge that Dowden's *Life of Shelley* is dictated by Lady Shelley, or even in any essential way influenced by her, is utterly false.

(4) *That Lady Shelley failed to print in* Shelley and Mary *true copies of the original MSS.*

The constant implications are that Lady Shelley deliberately omitted or altered ("bowdlerized") significant passages so that any biographer depending upon the text would be led to make serious errors or misinterpretations. I contend that this charge also is essentially not true. Professor Smith gives the impression that the Shelley MSS have never been seen and that no means of establishing the validity of the *Shelley and Mary* texts are available. This is far from being the case. There is no need to enlarge especially upon this point since Dowden's *Life of Shelley*, until recently the keystone of modern Shelley scholarship, has already been shown to be reliably based on the original MSS, but a few facts may be helpful.

Lady Shelley divided her collection into three portions: one portion went to the Bodleian Library (received 13 June 1893); another to the heir of the family title; and a third to her adopted daughter. These portions, each a considerable collection in itself, are now in the possession of the Bodleian, Sir John Shelley-Rolls, and the present Lord Abinger.[26a]

---

[26] *Letters of Edward Dowden and His Correspondents*, p. 221.

[26a] Since this article appeared in 1946, Sir John Shelley-Rolls has presented his collection to the Bodleian, and Lord Abinger has opened his collection to a number of scholars who have been permitted to microfilm considerable portions of it.

The Bodleian MSS have been examined by many people. First of all, they have been thoroughly catalogued. Mr. R. H. Hill, of the Bodleian staff, edited *The Shelley Correspondence in the Bodleian Library* in 1926. The following from Mr. Hill's Introduction (pp. iv-v) is well worth quoting:

After the centenary of Shelley's death, at the request of the Curators, the Merton Professor of English Literature [George Stuart Gordon] and Mr. H. F. B. Brett-Smith, M.A., very kindly undertook an examination of the reserved papers, *collated the greater part of them with printed texts* [italics mine], and furnished the Curators with a detailed report . . . "It is clear," to quote the report mentioned above, "that Dowden, when he wrote his *Life of Shelley*, had all, or nearly all this material before him, and that with very few exceptions he printed everything that seemed to him of any importance. . . . The chief value of the collection is in the material which it contains for the correction and amplification of letters already published, should a final edition of Shelley's correspondence ever be attempted." [As it was in the Julian Edition.] It should be added that, except for the earlier letters (1810-14), the correspondence is nearly all included in the volumes of *Shelley and Mary*. . . .

It will be seen that most of the material sent to the Bodleian by Lady Shelley has been for some time already available for students, and that (perhaps with minor limitations) the greater part of the correspondence had already been freely placed at Professor Dowden's disposal. The correspondence here printed, while it serves to emphasize and to throw into somewhat greater relief the lights and shadows which in such rapid succession enveloped the Shelley family, can hardly be said to affect the known facts of Shelley's biography to any great degree.

Roger Ingpen collated all the Bodleian's Shelley letters for his Julian Edition of Shelley's Correspondence. Professor Newman I. White for his *Shelley* (1940), Miss R. Glynn Grylls for her *Mary Shelley* (1938), and Professor Elizabeth Nitchie—all these have, to my knowledge, examined the MSS or considerable portions of them. The MSS of Shelley's poetry have been examined and the careful results published by C. D. Locock in *An Examination of the Shelley Manuscripts in the Bodleian Library* (Clarendon Press, 1903). A. H. Koszul's *Shelley's Prose in the Bodleian Manuscripts* was published in 1910. I myself have transcribed the ninety-four letters of Mary Shelley for my *Letters of Mary W. Shelley* (1944). Sixty-six of these letters are printed in *Shelley and Mary*, and I have collated these texts with the original MSS. In 1944 I printed this comment: "*Shelley and Mary* was, of course, the chief source for Dowden's *Life of Shelley* and Marshall's *Life and Letters* [*of Mary Shelley*]. With reference to the letters which they print from that source, it is worth noting that, though in a few instances Dowden corrects his text from the original letters, Marshall depends entirely upon the book . . . The texts in *Shelley and Mary*, though not always accurate or complete, are on the whole fairly good."[27] I took pains to make this statement because, remembering Dowden's note of alarm about the inaccuracy of *Shelley and Mary*, I was expecting very bad texts, and was surprised to find them for all essential purposes quite adequate. The Bodleian MSS, though they have afforded many minor additions and corrections to the *Mary and Shelley* texts, have yielded nothing that seriously threatens the validity of *Shelley and Mary*.

As for the MSS now in the possession of Sir John Shelley-Rolls, they too have been examined. Sir John himself, who in no way shares the prejudices of Lady Jane Shelley, has given much attention to them, and in 1934 he and Roger Ingpen edited together a small volume of additional unpublished fragments entitled *Verse and Prose from the Manuscripts of P. B. Shelley*. Roger Ingpen also collated all the Shelley letters in this collection for his Julian Edition and has made extensive use of the MSS for other purposes. Sir

[27] *Letters of Mary W. Shelley*, I, xxv.

John gave me transcripts of his 122 Mary Shelley letters which he himself prepared from the original letters.

The Abinger collection alone has been virtually inaccessible. Even that has been examined, however, and used to a limited extent. Miss R. Glynn Grylls was permitted to use it in preparation for her *Mary Shelley*. Moreover, she handled, examined, and collated in part the precious Journal, about which Professor Smith is so much concerned. Miss Grylls describes the five volumes on pp. 273-275 of her book. Her use of this wonderful opportunity is very interesting. It is surely significant that of the twelve unpublished extracts which she prints from the original Journal, eleven of them are from the years after Shelley's death. The one extract within Shelley's lifetime (p. 119) shows only the addition of one sentence, which reads: "I now begin a new year—may it be a happier one than the last unhappy one [Mary is the writer]."[28]

On p. 160 Miss Grylls does a great favor by showing us the textual differences between Marshall (equivalent, almost, of *Shelley and Mary*) and the original Journal for a long passage of thirty-one printed lines. Here are the results: "dancing and music" omitted; "swiftly" for "swift"; "sensations" for "sentiments"; "make" for "makes"; "time" for "Time." On p. 49 Miss Grylls takes the journal entry for May 13, 1815, directly from the original MS. The only differences noticeable are Lady Shelley's substitution of the full name "Charles Clairmont" for "C.C." and her misreading of "The Pecksie, Dormouse" as "the Pecksie's doom slave"— a sad but harmless error. From considerable experience I know that these are typical examples of the difference between

[28] Miss Grylls labels the whole extract from the Journal as an "Unpublished entry," as she always does for anything printed only in *Shelley and Mary*. Only the sentence quoted is not in *Shelley and Mary*. The extract is dated Dec. 31, 1819.

the *Shelley and Mary* texts and the original MSS. This is why Dowden said, "wherever I looked" *Shelley and Mary* "is a far from accurate rendering of the MSS"—and also why he was willing to proceed almost to the end of the *Life* before he made the necessary collation with the MSS.

Professor Smith's alarm over the possibility of the Journal having been "bowdlerized" and altered and suppressed in important parts also exhibits his very imperfect acquaintance with the nature of the Journal. It was by no means the repository of Shelley and Mary's feelings and thoughts, but a record first of all of what they read. Where they went and what they did and saw is recorded in the fewest possible words, and a comment beyond the fact is a rare occurrence. There was no occasion for Lady Shelley to suppress any part of it, for it had almost nothing to relate about the inner personal lives of the Shelleys. Mary wrote the whole Journal except for a very few entries by Shelley. She was the daughter of William Godwin, and doubtless knew the kind of diary her father kept. Mary's Journal was not so brief and condensed as her father's, but it is almost as impersonal. Who can find anything to suppress in an entry like this, which is typical: "Sunday, Mar. 25 [1821].—Read Greek. Call on Emilia Viviani, along with Williams. The Opera in the evening, with Williams and Lauretta. A fine day."[29] The missing

---

[29] *Shelley and Mary*, III, 595.—Though T. J. Hogg's description of the Journal (Preface to his *Life of Shelley*) is not strictly accurate, it confirms what I have said about it: ". . . from the 28th of July, 1814, until a few days before his death, Shelley [and Mary] kept regularly a journal of his daily life, recording, day by day, all [certainly not all] that he did, read, and wrote; mentioning the letters received and sent by himself, the places which he visited, and the persons whom he saw. . . . Many pages are little more than dates, lists of books, and names of places and persons, but much curious matter is interspersed."

[My edition of *Mary Shelley's Journal* (Norman: University of Oklahoma Press) was published in September 1947. The preface gives a fuller analysis of the nature and contents of the Journal.]

leaves from the 1815 volume may possibly have contained facts which Mary did not wish to survive her. This, however, is purely conjecture, and will probably always remain conjecture. One does, of course, regret this loss, and the loss of the volume for May 14, 1815–July 20, 1816. It is not true, however, that Mary kept her Journal every day. There are many instances of her allowing it to lapse, most noticeably (for two months) after the death of William in 1819.

Professor Smith's suspicions of the unreliability of *Shelley and Mary*, and consequently of Lady Shelley, are not justified by the facts. If the original Journal is ever published, he will be greatly disappointed.[29a]

III. *An Account of the History of Shelley Forgeries, Especially of the Activities of the Master Forger, Major George Gordon Byron.*

This part of *The Shelley Legend* (pp. 36-83) is not in itself objectionable; in fact, it is useful. It begins with a brief discourse on handwriting generally and proceeds to an analysis of the handwriting of Shelley and those of his circle. The intervening discussion of the Harvard Shelley Notebook may be useful to the student, but can offer little to the Shelley scholar. As the account itself unintentionally shows, the services of a handwriting expert were not necessary to straighten out the blunderings of Woodberry in identifying Mary and Shelley's hands in his facsimile reprint of the Notebook. Without boasting I may say that I had straightened them out for myself long before I had read the conclusions of Miss Darbishire or of Marcel Kessel.

The materials for the chapter on handwriting were supplied by Mr. Louis A. Waters, a handwriting expert em-

---

[29a] It may be worth recording that H. B. Forman also collated some of the original MSS while they were in Lady Shelley's possession. See his *Prose Works of Shelley* (1880), IV, 343, note 1.

ployed by Professor Smith for the purpose of identifying Shelley forgeries. No one will quarrel with Professor Smith for this procedure, except to suggest that it would have been helpful to have had two experts. I do not even propose to quarrel with Professor Smith about the method in which he supplied Mr. Waters with materials. It is nevertheless true that his method, on which he is vague, is very questionable. Apparently Mr. Waters never saw an original Shelley MS, and had to depend entirely on photostats; and any investigator can tell you that photostats are wholly inadequate for decisive judgments on many details. Apparent, too, is the fact that the chief examples of Shelley's handwriting examined by Mr. Waters were those found in the Harvard Shelley Notebook. It is never pointed out by Professor Smith that this Notebook contains only fair copies of Shelley's poems, and is therefore in no way useful for a study of Shelley's usual off-handwriting.

The Shelley Legend proceeds next to an account of the career of Major Byron, the forger of many Shelley, Keats, and Byron letters. The account is interesting and helpful, and I could even thank the author for it if it were not used later for reprehensible purposes. It should be made clear, however, that this account is, except for a few items, merely an expansion of materials already published by Seymour De Ricci, Samuel C. Chew, and myself.[30]

---

[30] Seymour De Ricci, *A Bibliography of Shelley's Letters*, Privately Printed, 1927, pp. 293-295 and at various places throughout the book. Samuel C. Chew, *Byron in England*, London, 1924, pp. 187-190. *The Letters of Mary W. Shelley*, II, 263-270, 294-296.—It is true that the author convicts me of having made some errors in printing the correspondence of Mary Shelley which relates to Major Byron:—the erroneous combination of the parts of three letters, the incorrect dating of some undated letters, and in consequence the duration of Mary's dealings with the forger and the extent of her purchases from him. But he has in no way changed the validity of my conclusions that Major Byron unquestionably had a considerable quantity of genuine Shelley letters, that he would not have dared

We are told how for a considerable period in 1845 and 1846 Mary Shelley, through Thomas Hookham, purchased from Major Byron an indeterminate quantity of Shelley's and her own letters; and that later Sir Percy and Lady Shelley purchased at public auction and possibly privately letters which proved to be forgeries. We also get the story of the publication by Moxon in 1852 of the volume entitled *The Letters of P. B. Shelley*, with an Introductory Essay by Robert Browning, the public excitement created by the immediate discovery that the letters were forgeries, an analysis of the sources of the forger's texts, and various other details, including the Hodges sale of seven Shelley letters and one MS, mostly forgeries, in December 1848.

The important thing to notice with reference to this part of *The Shelley Legend* is that it offers little not already well known to Shelley scholars and collectors. In fact, the forgeries of Shelley letters are exceptionally well known, thanks to the prolonged and scholarly work of Seymour De Ricci.

The purpose of the analysis of Major Byron's career, however, is not the legitimate one of informing the public on a matter known mainly to scholars only, but to lay the foundation for the later charges, given in the main by suggestion and insinuation rather than by direct statement:—that the Shelley family have both unintentionally and purposely used forgeries in their possession as genuine documents; and that many Shelley forgeries are still at large.

IV. *The New Forgeries.*

If Professor Smith had dropped the subject of forgeries

---

try to sell forgeries to Mary, who, better than any handwriting expert in the world, could have detected forgeries of Shelley's or her own letters. He might have offered to sell "copies," but Mary was obviously not interested in these. My errors, due mainly to the use of microfilms, are in themselves a good example of the danger of working with reproductions of MSS instead of with the originals.

after reviewing Major Byron's career, his book would not have created the sensation it was obviously intended to create. After so elaborate a preparation, however, he feels obliged to show the fruits of his labors. This he proceeds to do by claiming to have discovered hitherto unsuspected forgeries. And it is in this way, and in this alone, that he succeeds in giving a spurious validity to his claims that Shelley scholarship is not on a sound basis. He rightly thinks that if in so short a time, and with so inadequate a preparation, and with virtually no access to original MSS, he can shock the public with proof that some important Shelley documents are forgeries, he can make the public think that the undiscovered forgeries are legion and that nothing is dependable as genuine evidence.

Professor Smith never summarizes for the reader precisely what he has proved or attempted to prove. Out of the confusion of details, mixed with constant repetitions of the deficiencies of Dowden and Newman White and of the dishonesty of Mary and Lady Shelley, I shall extract Professor Smith's claims of new discoveries of forgery, and then discuss them. I warn the reader in advance that I do not think *The Shelley Legend* establishes a single forgery not heretofore clearly identified.

It is rather surprising, after wading through fifty-five pages of *The Shelley Legend,* to find that Professor Smith claims, as new, no more than this: (1) that the long-suspected Wise copy of one Shelley letter is a forgery; (2) that two other Shelley letters, hitherto unsuspected, are forgeries; (3) that the concluding lines of a third Shelley letter, hitherto unsuspected, are a forgery; (4) that one Mary Shelley letter should be suspected as a forgery; and (5) that one Shelley MS is a forgery. Here are the five letters and one MS:

1. Shelley to Mary, December 16, 1816 (Wise copy)

(pp. 84-109)

The results of Professor Smith's assiduous search for forgeries are rather slender, and if he succeeded in establishing all the above as forgeries in the particular copies he studies, the effects on Shelley biography would be slight. But the implications would be serious—and it is these which Professor Smith is eager to establish, for on them depends the existence of his "Shelley Legend."

One thing should be made clear at once. Though a great display has been made concerning handwriting, only two of the six so-called forgeries are in any way connected with the opinion of Mr. Waters, the handwriting expert; namely, Nos. 1 and 6. Proofs of the others as forgeries are arrived at purely by reasoning from facts, the connection or interpretation of which is extremely tenuous. In none of the six cases has the original MS been examined.

1. *Shelley to Mary, December 16, 1816 (Wise Copy).*

Professor Smith chooses this particular document as the foundation for his building of forgeries. Upon it he expends time, space, and photographic reproductions. It is his fond belief that if he can prove the Wise copy of Shelley's letter a forgery, he can prove that there were no charges against Harriet: "The importance of this letter to Shelley biography must not be underestimated, for upon a single paragraph in it *depends* one of the major charges against Harriet Westbrook (Shelley's first wife) as a prostitute, and her sister Eliza as a murderess" (p. 84). When Professor Smith finds several other letters which contradict his assertion, he is forced to say that they too are forgeries. When he is done, however, he has found no explanation for half a dozen other sources of the story about Harriet, sources which he himself quotes.

Professor Smith is also forced to assert that, granting the Wise letter a forgery, there was no original of which it was a true copy. Even Professor Smith, though constantly asserting that the letter in all its versions is wholly false, finds it hard to avoid the truth. "If, then," he says (pp. 85-86), "the Wise holograph . . . can be proved a forgery, Shelley's responsibility for this dubious letter disappears, *unless there exists somewhere an undisclosed original* [italics mine]. Certainly all the known manuscript versions . . . are forgeries. We cannot, therefore, without evidence of an original, accept Professor White's evasion of these difficulties by stating that critics agree that the forgeries of this letter are based on an original. (White, I. p. 723, n. 45.)" On p. 304 Professor Smith is not quite so sure of this: "Professor White may be quite right in his assumption without proof that back of the crucial December 16 and January 11 and other Harriet letters there lie genuine originals." As for the December 16 letter, there is proof enough: Mary Shelley answers it point by point in her letter of December 17, 1816, and as Professor Smith himself proves, it is the Wise version that she answers.

Professor Smith also admits that Garnett, H. B. Forman, Wise, Ingpen, De Ricci, and White—a formidable array of names in Shelley scholarship—are all positive that the Wise letter is the genuine original. Arrayed against the authenticity of the letter are honorable names, but not of the same potency: Edmund Blunden, Sylva Norman, and Alfred Pollard. These argue only from internal evidence, never having seen the MS itself, whereas all those for the MS have examined it carefully, except possibly White.

Professor Smith's additions to the history of the letter (pp.

91-96), from papers recently become available in the Berg Collection of the New York Public Library, are welcome indeed. But unfortunately they do not support his case. They prove, in fact, that in 1867 John Tilley, Secretary of the General Post Office, London, was convinced that the letter was a genuine original. And Tilley is most unlikely to be wrong about post office procedure and postmarks in 1859, Mr. Pollard to the contrary notwithstanding. A still stronger fact is that H. B. Forman, fully aware of Lady Shelley's belief that the letter was a forgery, and after examining the letter, bought it for £21. He backed up his opinion with his money.

This brings us to the only fact that looks at first glance like a serious confirmation of Professor Smith's claim that the Wise copy is a forgery;—namely, Lady Shelley's emphatic statement to Spencer Shelley in 1867 that it was a forgery. It is easy enough to explain how she came to make this mistake, but of course Professor Smith is not interested in finding an explanation, for it would destroy his case.

As Lady Shelley herself has stated in *Shelley Memorials* and elsewhere, she was painfully aware of the existence of forgeries of this and other letters, for she and Sir Percy had already purchased several which they had identified as forgeries because they had the original in their possession. In fact, by 1867 she must have been pretty well fed up with forgeries of this letter. When, therefore, she received from Spencer Shelley a copy of the December 16, 1816 letter which had been sent to him by Tilley, she instantly thought it another forgery. It never occurred to her that through error a Shelley letter in her possession could have got into the mail again in 1859. These two facts (not called to our attention by Professor Smith) must not be overlooked: (1) Lady Shelley never saw the MS she was so confidently calling a forgery (Spencer Shelley sent only a copy—see p. 92); had she seen it, she would doubtless have changed her mind at once. (2)

Lady Shelley was absolutely unaware that the letter posted again in 1859 and called to her attention by Spencer Shelley had ever been in her possession. If this had been known to her, she would have said so, have requested its return (even if it had been one of the forged copies), and then tried to discover how it got posted again. That this copy of the letter had been in her hands is proved by Professor Smith himself, who points out that Garnett had copied from it while it was in her possession "the passage partly torn by the seal" (p. 93), a circumstance which forced him to fill in by conjecture the obliterated words. Garnett's having quoted from this copy is also proof that he considered it the genuine original. Granting her ignorance of these facts, it is not difficult to understand Lady Shelley's positive assertion that the letter called to her attention by Spencer Shelley was a forgery.

It still remains, of course, that Lady Shelley got the MSS mixed and made the further error of printing the *Shelley and Mary* text from the forged copy, and of defending the forged copy as the original. This is regrettable, but since the deceptive forgery was a "true copy nevertheless," no great harm was done.

In tracing the history of the forged copy which Lady Shelley defended and the Wise copy which somehow got posted again in 1859 (though Lady Shelley never knew this), Professor Smith makes the absolutely unwarranted (and certainly unprovable) statement (p. 97) that the Wise copy was purchased at the 1851 sale, and the forged copy was sold to Mary Shelley by Major Byron in 1845-46. He completely overlooks the fact that Lady Shelley had in her possession at least three copies of this letter: two forgeries which were determined to be forgeries by the fact that the original was in their possession.[31] If Mary Shelley got this letter from Major

---

[31] Lady Shelley wrote, "Twice have forgeries of these very letters been brought to us and twice we have bought them." Quoted on p. 92 of *The Shelley Legend.*

Byron in 1845-46, she got the original letter, and the probabilities still are that this is the much-debated Odyssey letter in the Wise Collection.

The proof of forgery by handwriting tests (pp. 100-109), I do not propose to argue. I simply believe Mr. Waters is quite mistaken. If he and other handwriting experts should examine the original MS and pronounce it a forgery, proving at the same time that they are sufficiently acquainted with a reasonable variety of original Shelley MSS, I would bow to their opinion. In the meanwhile, Forman's willingness to back the genuineness of the letter with £21 in 1908 is a much more powerful argument.

My own conclusion is that Professor Smith has by no means proved the Wise letter a forgery.

2. *Mary to Shelley, December 17, 1816.*

Professor Smith has grave difficulties with this letter, for he knows that it authenticates the Wise letter. He makes a valiant effort to turn up some evidence, but his strongest evidence is his flat assertion (several times) that the Wise letter is a forgery: "Mary's reply, moreover, dovetails not with this Lady Shelley-Dowden version [of the December 16 letter], but with the Wise forgery" (p. 110). He tries hard to prove that there were variant copies, but admits manfully that "These changes may be editorial ones" (p. 111). He even tries to show that Mary exhibited too much knowledge of law when she advised "Shelley about Westbrook's lawyer, Desse, as though she were experienced in legal processes of procrastination" (p. 111).

This is rather pitiful and would never have been written by Professor Smith if he could have avoided it. But he had to say something about this troublesome letter. When that duty is accomplished, however, he promptly forgets it and goes blithely on assuring us that the Wise letter is a forgery.

He makes his conclusion as strong as possible, but this is the best he can do:

The authenticity of this letter, therefore, may remain suspect until the only extant manuscript version in the Bodleian can be subjected to a handwriting examination in order to disclose whether the autograph is Mary's or Major Byron's; or until a genuine original . . . is brought to light. Should it prove to be Mary's the question would then arise, did she write it in 1816, or 1845-50? (pp. 111-112).

The last sentence I shall comment on later. All that needs to be added here is that if this letter is a forgery, it is the first Mary Shelley forgery on record. And finally, that I myself saw the MS in the Bodleian in 1937 and transcribed the text for my edition of *The Letters of Mary W. Shelley*.

In this case, then, Professor Smith has proved nothing beyond the fact that Mary's letter of December 17, 1816, is for him a stumbling block.

3. *Shelley to Mary, January 11, 1817.*

Professor Smith's proof that this letter is a forgery consists entirely of an attempt, through catalogue descriptions, to identify two versions of the letter known to have been in Lady Shelley's possession (Bodleian and Shelley-Rolls copies) with a forgery bought by Evans for Mary Shelley at the Hodges sale on 18 December 1848 and with a forgery bought by Hookham for Sir Percy and Lady Shelley at the White sale on 12 May 1851. His contention is that when the White letter came into Lady Shelley's possession in 1851, she pronounced it a forgery because she already had from Mary the Hodges letter, also a forgery but mistaken by her for the original.

The case appears to be strengthened by the fact that Lady Shelley used a forged copy for the *Shelley and Mary* text, and that in his *Life* Dowden also printed from the forged

document, which differs slightly from the letter in the possession of Sir John Shelley-Rolls, now claimed by Sir John and
Roger Ingpen to be the authentic original letter. The Bodleian copy, which apparently was used by Lady Shelley, has
been pronounced by the competent authority of Mr. R. H.
Hill, then Secretary of the Bodleian, as a forgery. Professor
Smith makes much of the fact that Ingpen changed his mind
about the authenticity of the Bodleian copy after Mr. Hill
pronounced it a forgery and after Ingpen had examined the
Shelley-Rolls copy in or about 1934. Ingpen had had little
reason to suspect the Bodleian copy, but after it was questioned it can be assumed that he examined Sir John's copy
with great care.

Again it must be admitted that Lady Shelley got her MSS
mixed. Also that Dowden was deceived, for he printed, not
from the *Shelley and Mary* text but from the MS itself.
Moreover, Dowden found among the MSS an extra leaf belonging to this letter but not associated with it either by him
or by Lady Shelley. Dowden printed the extra leaf as a separate letter, as did Ingpen; but it does not appear in *Shelley
and Mary* at all.[32]

Professor Smith never admits, of course, that the identification of unseen MSS purely by catalogue entries and by other
inferences[33] is at the best far from reliable as definitive evidence. He also fails again to admit the very evident fact that
Lady Shelley had more than two copies of the letter, one of
which might well have been the genuine original. Again, too,
he gives no credence to the fact that even if all known copies
are forgeries, a true original may very well have been the
basis of the forgeries.

[32] This is but one more of numerous details which prove that Dowden
did see the original MSS.

[33] For instance, that after Mary's death Lady Shelley found the Hodges
forgery in a packet of letters marked "Shelley letters" (p. 120).

Two matters of importance Professor Smith overlooks entirely. His claim that Sir John Shelley-Rolls's copy, now claimed by Ingpen to be the original, is identical with the 1851 forgery is based on the identical descriptions of the MS in 1851 and 1934, as consisting of 5 pages. Ingpen[34] describes the Shelley-Rolls MS as "six quarto pages." When Ingpen adds that "the second part, which was printed for the first time by Dowden, consists of two pages . . . it bears on the back the address and the postmark," Professor Smith concludes (p. 121) that the MS was actually 5 pages. This is a treacherous argument because Ingpen was himself a bookseller and knew perfectly well how to describe MSS. It is well known that the page which has "the address and the postmark" may at the same time have, on the parts which are folded under when it is addressed and mailed, a considerable amount of writing.

Professor Smith also fails to point out a very significant entry in Mary's Journal. On January 12[–15][35] she wrote: "Four days of idleness. Letters from Shelley; he is obliged to stay in London." Now when one turns to Shelley's letter of January 11, he finds that Shelley takes pains to explain why he must remain in London for some time:

On the 19th the Chancellor begins to sit . . . I know not when, or whether at all, before that day I can return to Bath. How painful in these difficult, and in one sense tremendous circumstances it is to me to be deprived of the counsel of your judgment and the consolation of your dear presence. I must remain in London—I must attend to every, the minutest stage of the answer which is to be drawn up on my side."[36]

[34] *Verse and Prose from the MSS. of P. B. Shelley*, ed. Shelley-Rolls and Ingpen, p. 134.

[35] One entry for four days. Claire's baby, Allegra, was born on January 12. *Shelley and Mary*, I, 178.

[36] Julian Edition, IX, 216.

Professor Smith has not proved that Shelley did not write the January 11, 1817 letter. Mary Shelley has given a decisive answer to that. Neither has he proved that Sir John Shelley-Rolls's MS is not the original letter, as Sir John and Ingpen both think it is.

4. *Shelley to Byron, January 17, 1817.*

Professor Smith says positively that "this is another forgery which has crept back into Shelley biography as an authentic letter. When the present owner, who now refuses, permits the holograph itself to be submitted to unbiased examination and publication it will be found a production of Major Byron's pen" (p. 131).

The proof of forgery rests on three points. First, that the letter "is not addressed on the outside (Ingpen, IX, 220). Byron was in Italy at this time, Shelley was in London, and the letter . . . seems not to have been sent through the mails, for Ingpen lists no postmark as he does for letters bearing postmarks" (p. 130). Though not important in themselves, these difficulties are easily removed.

On January 13, 1817, at Bath, Mary Shelley wrote to Lord Byron a letter of that date apprising him of the birth of Allegra on January 12. On the same date she wrote a note to Mrs. Leigh Hunt. Though the letter is lost, it is quite apparent that she wrote Shelley on the same day. In her letter to Shelley she enclosed the note to Mrs. Hunt, which is merely addressed "Mrs. Hunt" (Shelley was staying with the Hunts), and the letter to Byron, for Shelley's inspection. Shelley himself wrote to Byron on January 17 and enclosed his letter in Mary's, which is addressed "To the Right Honourable/ Lord Byron/ M. Hentsch-Banquier/ Genêve/ Switzerland," and has the postmarks (1) E/PAID/ 18 JA 18/ 1817 and (2) F 19 17.[37]

[37] *Letters of Mary W. Shelley*, I, 17-18.

The letter was sent to Byron at Geneva because the Shelleys thought he was still there. Even when Shelley wrote again on April 23 he did not know Byron's address ("Rumour says that you are at Venice"). Still not hearing from Byron, Shelley wrote again on July 9. It was not until September that a letter from Byron finally arrived, as Shelley's letter of September 24 indicates.[38] If the letter of January 17 is a forgery, so is the letter of April 23, which very clearly refers to the January 17 letter; in fact, the whole series would have to be forgeries![39]

Professor Smith's second point is that there appear to be variant versions, which would therefore prove the existence of a forgery. He claims that *Shelley and Mary* "includes a part-sentence [italicized below] . . . not to be found in Murray or in the Julian edition" (p. 128). *Shelley and Mary* reads (I, 181–182):

So here is an imperfect account of my misfortunes (yet one thing happened in the autumn that affected me far more deeply), *which you must suppose to mean, not that I wish to trouble you with them or interest you in them; but that I wish to say,* 'I should have written to you before if I had been beaten down by any common griefs.'

Here is the history of the texts referred to by Professor Smith. Lady Shelley copied the letter for *Shelley and Mary* from the MS owned by Lady Dorchester, from whom it passed later to John Murray. In 1922 John Murray printed it in *Lord Byron's Correspondence,* transcribing it from the same original MS, and through an inadvertence omitting the part-sentence. Ingpen published the letter in the Julian Edi-

---

[38] On Friday, September 19, 1817, Mary wrote in her Journal: "Letter from Albe [i.e., Byron]" (*Shelley and Mary,* I, 217). The entry obviously covers the period September 2-19; on September 2 Mary's baby Clara was born.

[39] These letters to Byron are in the Julian Edition, IX, 218-220, 226-227, 232-233, 245-247.

tion, taking his text from *Lord Byron's Correspondence*, not from the original, which he never saw. All the letters to Byron are taken by him from Murray's book, and all of them lack the address and postmarks because these are not printed by Murray.

Professor Smith's third point is a question as to the provenance of the letter. He attempts to show that John Cam Hobhouse, Lord Brougham, who gave the letter, with others, to Lady Dorchester, his sister, could in one way or another have come into possession of Major Byron forgeries. Not a grain of evidence is offered, and no consideration is given to the fact that Hobhouse was not only one of Byron's most intimate friends, but also one of the executors of his estate, which circumstances would give him many opportunities of acquiring Byron letters and MSS.

Once more Professor Smith has failed to prove his case, and once again his defeat is attributable mainly to evidence given by Mary Shelley.

5. *Shelley to Mary, [November 4, 1814]—Concluding lines only.*

Professor Smith's claims with reference to this letter are relatively mild. His only contention is that the last lines, beginning "Thus it is my letters are full of money," are forged. He shows that through the Hodges sale of 1848 Mary Shelley secured a one-page MS which began with the words just quoted, assumes that Lady Shelley regarded the MS as authentic and tacked it on as the concluding lines to an incomplete genuine letter in her possession, and printed the two as one letter in *Shelley and Mary*.

There are six deficiencies in this story: (1) the assumption that Lady Shelley did not have the complete original MS in her possession. This could easily be the case even under Professor Smith's theory, which does not question the validity of the greater part of the letter. (2) The assumption that Lady Shelley thought the fragment from the Hodges sale genuine, which though possible cannot be assumed. (3) The assumption that the Hodges sale fragment was a forgery. The 1851 White letter on the same subject was a forgery, and was immediately identified as such; but it has never been proved that the Hodges Shelley letters were all forgeries. (4) The assumption that the Hodges fragment, if granted to be a forgery, was not a true copy of an authentic letter. (5) The assumption that Lady Shelley, in attaching the concluding lines, could not tell by the MS that the two fragments were parts of one letter. (6) And finally, the assumption that "A careful reader of the letter . . . will observe that the painful financial and private details which Shelley relates to Mary in the first four paragraphs cease abruptly" (p. 126), and that therefore the two fragments do not match. If the "careful reader" cannot see a beautiful transition in "Thus it is my letters are full of money," he may be "careful" but he is certainly not intelligent. The following extract, which gives only part of the financial details, shows how the two parts fit together. I have italicized the first words of the portion which Professor Smith claims to be a forgery.

Hookham has been with me. I do not despair of arranging something with Charles, so that £100 may be placed at my disposal. Hookham is to meet me with Charles on 'Change tomorrow. I shall previously have disposed of Ballachy to my purpose, and entertain some confidence of success. H. seems interested in the affair. Mrs. B. will go to the London Coffee House tomorrow and call for my letters. I hope to hear from Sir John. Mrs. Stewart's affair, which I have most of all at heart—that relentless enemy of all comfort—remains as it did. H. urges Tahourdin to complete it; but she will not at present. I expect to hear from Hooper tomorrow. *Thus it is my letters are full of money,* whilst my being overflows with unbounded love and elevated thoughts. How little philosophy and affection consort with this turbid scene—this dark

scheme of things finishing in unfruitful death! There are moments in your absence, my love, when the bitterness with which I
regret the unrecoverable time wasted in unprofitable solitude and
worldly cares is a most painful weight; you alone reconcile me to
myself and to my beloved hopes.

Good night, my excellent love, my own Mary.[40]

Even with this unimportant fragment Professor Smith cannot prove his charge of forgery.

6. WISE MS OF *A Proposal for Putting Reform to the Vote.*

The forgery here proclaimed by Professor Smith has no
biographical significance since there is no question of Shelley's
having written and published in 1817 the pamphlet entitled
*A Proposal for Putting Reform to the Vote Throughout the
Kingdom.* Professor Smith's main purpose seems to be the
creation of an opportunity to make sweeping and sensational
charges against Mr. Thomas J. Wise. If Mr. Wise had never
encountered more formidable opponents than Professor
Smith, his reputation today would be as sound as he himself
could have wished.

In spite of the fact that the Wise MS of *A Proposal* has, as
Professor Smith admits, a "water-tight authentication"—from
Shelley to Ollier (his publisher), to Ollier's family, to Mr.
Francis Harvey (bookseller) by public auction in July 1877,[41]
to T. J. Wise by purchase from Mr. Harvey—Professor
Smith pronounces it a forgery on the grounds of handwriting,
and then theorizes as to how Major Byron could have accom-
plished the feat.

The handwriting test I need say nothing about except that
to me it is not in the least convincing. The assertion that it
resembles the writing in the December 16, 1816 letter I will

[40] Dowden, *Life of Shelley*, I, 503-504.
[41] Professor Smith has 1879, in a faulty quotation (p. 291) from H. B.
Forman's Introduction to the Facsimile Reprint of the MS for the Shelley
Society, 1887, p. 9.

agree with; but since I do not believe that letter a forgery, the argument has no weight with me.

The following statement also shows that Professor Smith and Mr. Waters have tried to judge one Shelley MS by comparison with another Shelley MS which is in no way comparable:

The remarkable variation in the handwriting in the short space of sixteen and a quarter pages of this alleged pamphlet is in itself something to give one pause when it is contrasted with the uniformity of slant and proportions of the letters in the Harvard Notebook in poems like "A Vision of the Sea" and "Hymn to Mercury." (p. 292)

A Proposal is a rough draft written hurriedly, while the Harvard Notebook, as I have already pointed out, is made up entirely of fair copies, which would very naturally be more regular in style. Professor Smith evidently has no conception of the chaos of the notebooks in which Shelley originally wrote and corrected his poems.

I would also question as highly dubious the method by which Leigh Hunt's authentication of the sketch by Shelley on the back of p. 14 of the MS is pronounced a forgery (p. 293). My own reaction is one of considerable surprise at the close resemblance of the so-called forged authentication and the same words assembled from various Leigh Hunt MSS. The same words from other Leigh Hunt MSS would probably not resemble the chosen Leigh Hunt words as much as those already chosen resemble the so-called forgery.

Professor Smith also fails to tell us how Major Byron could have got his forged MS into the hands of Charles Ollier (died 1859) or of Ollier's family; and how Major Byron could have got hold of the proof sheets of the pamphlet which Leigh Hunt had in his possession and gave at some time to Sir Percy and Lady Shelley.

In fact, Professor Smith explains nothing. As for his claims about handwriting, I consider H. B. Forman a far better judge than Professor Smith or Mr. Waters, who have not even seen the original MS.

Once again Professor Smith has failed to substantiate his claim of having discovered a forgery.

I have, I believe, shown that Professor Smith has not been able to prove the existence of a single forgery not already known, and that in most cases there is not even a basis for suspicion. If this is true, I have also shown that his sensational charges that Shelley scholarship is not on a sound basis are wholly unfounded.

V. *That Mary and Lady Shelley Were in Collusion with a Forger.*

Professor Smith has charged Mary and Lady Shelley with collusion with Major Byron to produce forged letters which would prove Harriet's guilt and justify Shelley and Mary. He does not make the charges outright; but he makes them by indirect means at frequent intervals. When he says that a forger produced letters which were injurious to Harriet's and helpful to Shelley's reputation, he is at the same time making charges against Mary and Lady Shelley, for he knows as well as the reader that Major Byron had no personal interest whatsoever in the Harriet-Shelley-Mary Shelley affair, or in Shelley biography generally. If he manufactured such forgeries which were not copies of genuine letters, he did so because he was paid to do so. (What an opportunity for blackmail this would have afforded him!) The theme of *The Shelley Legend* is that Mary and Lady Shelley desired to defame Harriet and desired documentary evidence to prove her guilt.

There can be no question about the charges made, as the following excerpts sufficiently prove.

Should it [the Bodleian MS of Mary's letter of December 17,

1816, to Shelley] prove to be Mary's the question would then arise, did she write it in 1816, or 1845-50? (p. 112)

We shall never know the lengths to which the forger went to substantiate the conduct of Shelley and Mary as against that of Harriet ... We shall not go further than De Ricci, for want of evidence, in speculating how close were Mary's relations with this forger or how much he did her bidding or catered to her whims or suggestions. (p. 122)

It is significant that Lady Shelley in all her references to forged Shelley letters never mentions Major Byron, though he was publicly exposed in 1852, the year after she had bought forgeries of his at auction. (p. 123)

It will perhaps not be amiss to summarize here the case built up for Shelley and Mary by the forger in this letter [of December 16, 1816], which skilfully purveys exactly what Mary and her Shelley relatives wished to establish. (p. 102)

The fact that he [Shelley] used none of these charges is proof that he did not possess them (perhaps never knew them) and that their existence depends solely upon Godwin and Mary's allegations and upon the forged letters of December 16 and January 11 and January 17, which contain them—letters that probably did not exist before 1845. (p. 124)

... which shows that he [Peacock] was not, like Hunt, aware of Mary and Lady Shelley's purchase of the Major Byron forgeries and how their contents were being used. (p. 187)

... Dr. Garnett could not in the light of the mis-information, the false charges, and the forged letters supplied him by Lady Shelley form as correct an opinion of the separation as Peacock. (p. 191)

... in view of the Major's extensive activities as a blackmailer and extortioner, the Harriet letters may be his own clever compositions, which the Mary Shelley family bought and found "apt and of great credit." (p. 304)

That the charge against Mary Shelley is completely without foundation, and that Mary cannot even be suspected of collusion with a forger, is definitely proved by *The Shelley Legend* itself. The account (pp. 64–77) of her dealings with G. Byron through Thomas Hookham in 1845–46 is the one thing in the book which seems reasonably accurate, and it shows conclusively that Mary never saw Major Byron in person, never wished to see him, and was fully aware of his shady character. After she had succeeded in getting from him all the Shelley letters it seemed possible to get, and when it was evident that Byron had made copies and was threatening to sell them for publication, her inclination was to let him alone and merely to threaten to prosecute anyone who published them. When in 1849 she was notified by White of Shelley letters in his hands and Mary sent Hookham to discuss their purchase, she evidently considered this another threat to publish "copies," for "Hookham . . . read to White an extract from Mrs. Shelley's letter, 'couched in so angry and coarse a tone, as to leave no doubt that she thought my only motive,' White says, 'was to extort money.' " (*Shelley Legend*, p. 53.)

Neither in his treatment of Mary Shelley's life before 1845, nor in his account of her dealings with G. Byron, can Professor Smith establish the fact that Mary Shelley even desired to blacken Harriet's character. The only facts available prove conclusively that she defended Harriet from Hunt's misrepresentation in 1825.

The problem as to where Major Byron got the genuine Shelley and Mary letters which he undoubtedly possessed in 1845, and virtually all of which he evidently sold to Mary Shelley, may possibly have some further light shed on it. I have little doubt that what Moxon told White was essentially true: "he told White also of the box of letters which the Shelleys had left behind them at Marlow, and which the landlord (Maddocks) had sold to collect his arrears in rent, and that many of these 'lost letters' had fallen into the hands of a Mr. Byron, 'who had been troublesome to the family, in endeavouring to extort money for the purpose of suppressing them' " (p. 53). Certain it is that Mr. Madocks did have some Shelley documents, and that he had some as late as 1858, for Charles S. Middleton saw and used them for his *Shelley and His Writings* (1858), as his Preface testifies.

The "box" has usually been identified with Mary's desk, which Peacock sent to her in Italy; but it is by no means identical with the desk. When Mary finally received her desk at Genoa, she wrote in her Journal for October 7, 1822:

> I have received my desk today, and have been reading my letters to mine own Shelley during his absences at Marlow. What a scene to recur to! My William, Clara, Allegra, all are talked of. They lived then, they breathed this air . . .[42]

It is significant that she mentions only her letters, not Shelley's, which would have been infinitely more important to her, and which she would have read first.

This alone would indicate that Mary did not get all the letters left at Marlow. There is also evidence that she was keenly aware that many letters, especially Shelley's, were missing. She wrote Peacock urgently about papers left at Marlow, inquiring particularly about the missing letters. After considerable delay, Peacock wrote her on April 15, 1823, a full explanation of what had happened after the Shelleys left Marlow, and took care to answer her evidently persistent inquiries about lost letters.[43] According to Peacock, he had taken charge of the two writing desks, Shelley's (a large one), and Claire's (a small one), both of which were locked and were evidently full of papers—all, he had thought,

[42] *Shelley and Mary*, III, 884.
[43] *The Works of T. L. Peacock* (Halliford Edition), ed. by H. F. B. Brett-Smith and C. E. Jones (1934), VIII, 232-234.

of any consequence. Shelley's desk he had sent to Mary; Claire's he was holding.

Not Peacock, but Madocks, had supervised the packing and storage of Shelley's books and other personal property. Mr. Madocks had removed the books to his house. The new owner of Shelley's house, Mr. Carter, turned over to Peacock several packages containing papers and other items. Here Peacock says with emphasis that there were no letters in any of the packages. This may be perfectly true, but it is easily possible that the letters may have been packed with some of the books, or in a box which was removed by Madocks and never seen by Peacock. Peacock says, "I collected all the MSS that remained and sealed them in a parcel, *which I left in one of the boxes that are now with Maddocks.*"[43a] In other words, Mr. Madocks had everything except the two desks, which, as we know, did not contain the letters.

Moreover, Mr. Madocks had already shown a firm resolve to keep possession of Shelley's goods. Shelley wanted his books shipped to Italy early in 1822. This is what Peacock wrote to Shelley on February 28, 1822: "The boxes which I left with Maddocks he will not give up . . . he will not be satisfied with less than the total payment of your debt to him . . . he is determined to stand an action, with which he has been menaced, thinking perhaps that I shall not be willing to incur so great an expense."[43b]

These facts, then, are established: (1) Mary did not receive all the Marlow letters in Italy; (2) she was keenly aware of this and made special inquiries about them in 1822 and 1823; (3) Peacock had never seen them, and his story of how Shelley's possessions were handled by Mr. Madocks makes it evident that there could have been a box (or any number of boxes!) of letters which Peacock might well have known

[43a] *Ibid.,* p. 233.
[43b] *Ibid.,* p. 227.

nothing about; (4) Mr. Madocks was determined to keep Shelley's property until he was paid; (5) as late as 1858 he still had some Shelley papers. In the light of these facts it would seem that Major Byron (who did not know all these facts) was quite right in claiming that he got the letters from a "box" at Marlow. Nor should this fact be overlooked: Mayor Byron had Mary Shelley letters as well as Shelley letters. The former he rightfully (in view of the non-existent public demand for them) considered of little value and offered to "give" to Mary; he certainly would not have taken the trouble to forge them.

Professor Smith has not produced one shred of evidence to substantiate his charge against Mary Shelley—for charge it is; no evidence even for suspicion. He is still less successful with Lady Shelley, for he cannot establish any connection, or indication of connection, between Lady Shelley and Major Byron or any other forger.[43c] He can show only that Lady Shelley made a few (remarkably few) mistakes in arranging, transcribing, and printing a huge quantity of MSS, and that some two or three forged copies (on the whole "true copies nevertheless") did get mixed with the genuine MSS.

And that brings us to an important matter which Professor Smith has made no attempt to clarify because to do so would be to destroy his argument. The question is: Approximately how many forgeries did Lady Shelley have in her possession, and consequently to what extent could they vitiate Shelley biography if they were all accepted as genuine?

In 1845–46 Mary Shelley received from G. Byron an indeterminate quantity of Shelley and Mary letters, which must certainly have been genuine. The Shelley letters she evidently

---

[43c] Professor Smith fails to explain why Lady Shelley, if she were eager to establish charges against Harriet, omitted from her *Shelley and Mary* text of the January 11, 1817 letter the entire passage containing those charges.

tied together and marked "Shelley Letters," and this was doubtless the packet found by Lady Shelley after Mary's death.

Having exhausted his supply of genuine Shelley letters by sale to Mary, G. Byron began to produce forged Shelley letters, some of them being true copies of genuine letters which he had already disposed of, and some made up mainly of excerpts drawn from genuine letters already printed and from magazine articles. These forgeries he sold to White and others. The point to be stressed here is that some of the forgeries were true copies, and that those which were manufactured were innocuous biographically.

Now how many forgeries got into the Shelley archives? Granting that the five bought at the Hodges sale in 1848 were all forgeries (though this is not proved), there are five. In 1851 eleven forgeries were bought at the White sale—total sixteen. Lady Shelley wrote in 1867 that "Twice have forgeries of these very letters been brought to us and twice we have bought them" (*Shelley Legend*, p. 92). The quantity of "these very letters," the genuine letters, is unknown, but it probably corresponds pretty well with the eleven forgeries of the White sale. This then would make eleven more (the White Letters being included in the "Twice") or a total of twenty-seven forgeries. To be extremely generous, let us suppose that through other purchases the total of forgeries went up to fifty.

The effect on Shelley biography cannot, however, be estimated by the total number of forgeries, for these were more or less duplicates ("true copies") of genuine letters. Counting the genuine letters for the moment as copies, Lady Shelley then had three or four copies of each of from eleven to twenty letters. The point I am trying to make, even with numbers which I regard as grossly exaggerated, is that, though the number of forgeries may seem large, the number of individual letters forged is small. It may also be added that there is no reason to be greatly surprised if Lady Shelley, in dealing with a great quantity of MSS, and with forgeries which she confessed were often difficult to distinguish from genuine letters, —if she made a few errors. Professor Smith should be the last person to press charges of inaccuracy, for his *Shelley Legend* is filled with errors.

In making charges against Mary and Lady Shelley Professor Smith has allied himself with Trelawny, Jeaffreson, and Massingham; but these, I am sure, would spurn the alliance.

VI. *That the Truth about Claire Clairmont and Shelley has been Suppressed.*

This topic needs no discussion. Professor Smith is at liberty to believe whatever he pleases about the Hoppner affair and other things. These are mere matters of opinion on which he brings no new facts to bear. I do not accept any of his interpretations, but am in no way disturbed by them because Professor Smith is merely going over ground that has been covered many times before.

I believe I have disproved every important charge that Professor Smith has made which would indicate that Shelley scholarship is not on a sound basis. It now remains to point out, in addition to what has already been shown, a few of the countless errors which Professor Smith has made. Many of them are insignificant, but they do indicate that he is a novice in Shelley affairs and is incompetent to make any serious judgments with reference to Shelley.

1. Byron . . . veered off to Greece on the *Bolivar*. (p. 1)
[Byron sailed on the *Hercules*, having sold the *Bolivar* to Lord Blessington.]

2. Hither she [to Genoa Mary] brought her sole remaining

child, Percy Florence, but the Hunt ménage of bad housekeeping, financial chaos, and mischievous children who took delight in teasing young Percy, soon brought strained relations. (pp. 1-2)
[This is pure fancy; Mary got along very well with the Hunt family. The strained relations with Hunt were occasioned solely by Hunt's opinion, based mainly on misinformation given him by Jane Williams, that Mary had not made Shelley happy in recent years.]⁴⁴

3. Mary had assumed superintendence over the details of Shelley's life, forever going over his correspondence, commenting on it in postscripts, copying it in her own hand until Shelley in several letters was moved to express great annoyance at his wife's continual prying into his writings. (p. 2)
[This is simply not true. A few letters Mary did copy in order to compress them into smaller space and to save postage.]

4. Mary . . . whose quarrels with Medwin, Byron, and Guiccioli, and others of the Italian group, made Shelley's last years an intermittent hell. (p. 2)
[There is no evidence that Mary quarreled with any of these people.]

5. . . . after threats of suicide by both Harriet and Mary. (p. 3)
After threats of suicide by Mary. (p. 9)
[I believe the only basis for this is Harriet's letter of November 20 [1814] to Mrs. Nugent, questionable in itself as reliable evidence, but not capable even as it stands of being so construed: ". . . at last she [Mary] told him she was dying in love for him . . . She then told him she would die—he had rejected her." Printed in *The Shelley Legend* itself on p. 155.]

⁴⁴ Though the impressionistic purpose of the first paragraph (pp. 1-2) may be some excuse for the following statements, they are inappropriate in a book which supposedly is based on research and which announces important discoveries. The members of the old Pisa circle did not, of course, disperse themselves for any of the reasons assigned: "Trelawny . . . sailed away with Byron to assuage his own grief at the loss of the man he adored. The Countess Guiccioli after Byron's departure went away to her own consolations, for [because] she had never liked Mary or Claire Clairmont. Claire . . . drew away to Vienna to find a retreat for her sorrows."

6. But Mary's speedy repudiation of the life of this Italian set after Shelley's death is eloquent testimony that she did not belong in it and that she did not find these years in Italy the unadulterated bliss and harmony which her biographers have depicted. (p. 6)
[Instead of repudiating "this Italian set," Mary idealized it. Shelley's biographers have not so represented the Italian years, or the relationship of Shelley and Mary during those years.]

7. When she [Claire] gave birth in January, 1817, to Byron's child, Allegra, *the residents of Marlow wondered* and kept wondering until March 11, 1818, when the trio and children left for Italy. (p. 10)
[Allegra was born at Bath, not Marlow. Mary left Marlow on February 10, Shelley, Claire and the children having preceded her on February 7 and 9.]

8. His [Shelley's] friendship with the Gisbornes, especially Mrs. Gisborne, *succeeded* his interest in Sophia [November-December 1819]. (p. 10)
[Shelley's friendship with the Gisbornes began in 1818.]

9. The house would have had another occupant had Keats accepted Shelley's invitation of July 27 [1820]. (p. 10)
[Shelley's letter of [February 18, 1821] to Claire, shows that Shelley never meant that Keats should live in his own house: "Keats is very ill at Naples—I have written to him to ask him to come to Pisa, without however inviting him into our own house. We are not rich enough for that sort of thing."—Julian Edition, x, 242.]

10. Hunt an annuity in lieu of his £5,000. (p. 13)
[The sum should be £2,000.]

11. Mary reluctantly left Italy in 1823 for England to spare her child the pestilence of the Italian summer that had already robbed her of William and Clara. (p. 15)
[A half-truth; her chief purpose was to come to some arrangement with Sir Timothy.]

12. . . . the story Mary . . . had compelled the Hoppners and Byron to deny. (pp. 18-19)

[The Hoppners never denied the story, probably because they
never received Mary's letter, which was found among Byron's
papers at his death.]

13. The other drag [on Mary from 1822 on] was the per-
petually indigent Leigh Hunt . . . There was also her [Mrs.
Hunt's] bevy of *nine* incorrigible children whom Byron had
stigmatized as Yahoos . . . To keep such an establishment going
the large-hearted and patient Hunt looked to Mary for aid and
to the legacy Percy had left in his will. She rose bravely to meet
the occasion when he was importunate or brought along a solicitor
to represent his rights and demands. (pp. 19-20)
[The Hunts had six children when Byron so described them. Hunt
never thought of receiving any financial assistance from Mary
until Sir Timothy died in 1844. Shelley left no legacy to Hunt, but
Mary knew and informed Hunt of his intention to do so, and in
1844 honored that intention, for which there was no legal com-
pulsion.]

14. Shelley's Eton friend, Thomas Medwin. (p. 26)
[Medwin did not attend Eton; he was with Shelley at Sion House
Academy.]

15. Mary had bought the *seven* letters of the Hodges sale.
(p. 127)
[Evans bought for Mary only five of the seven letters.]

16. When *Shelley and Mary* appeared in 1882, only twelve
copies were allegedly printed, for private distribution among
Shelley's heirs and friends; one copy, however, came into the
possession of Lady Dorchester, who discovered that Lady Shelley
had committed a breach of trust by *publishing* in full the letter in
question [Shelley to Byron, January 17, 1817]. Lady Dorchester
thereupon threatened that, unless the entire edition were suppressed, she would ostracize Lady Shelley socially. . . . Lady Shelley
complied and withdrew the books. (p. 128)
["Publishing" should be "printing." Not only "the letter" but a
number of Shelley-to-Byron letters were printed in *Shelley and
Mary*, all from MSS owned by Lady Dorchester, who stipulated

that they were not to be published or quoted from. In each copy
of *Shelley and Mary* Lady Shelley wrote a note to that effect by
every letter concerned. I know of no basis for any threats by Lady
Dorchester or suppression and withdrawal of the books.]

17. Both letters should put an end, therefore, to the *Shelley
family fable* that Harriet and Shelley after prolonged estrangement
finding each other incompatible, *parted by mutual consent.*" (p.
156, repeated on p. 186)
[Mary expressly denied the "mutual consent" story in her letter
of December 28, 1825, to Hunt (printed in *The Shelley Legend*
on p. 21). Lady Shelley did not even allude to it in *Shelley
Memorials* or elsewhere in print. Garnett, unaware at the time
of Mary's denial, defended it to a limited extent in *Relics of
Shelley* (1862) on the basis of Hunt's published assertion in 1828,
of Shelley's Troyes letter to Harriet, and of his fairly amicable
relations with her in the autumn of 1814. Dowden rejected the
story.]

18. Professor Frederick L. Jones in an answer (*South Atlantic
Quarterly*, XLII, No. 4, Oct. 1943) [to J. H. Smith's "Shelley
and Claire Clairmont," PMLA, LIV, 785 ff.] has attempted a
refutation by quotations from the diaries. . . . Further, the statements in his two-volume *Letters of Mary Shelley* about this affair
grossly contradict his reply to J. H. Smith. (p. 158)
[In a seven-page article a group of quotations from the Journal
takes up less than one-half a page. The Journal is not utilized
further. There are no contradictory statements in my *Letters of
Mary Shelley*. The only statement relating to "this affair" is the
note (1, 7) which says that Claire's "presence had become unbear-
able to Mary," and that Claire "had been sent to Lynmouth."]

19. As late as January 1818 Shelley, in the following letter,
just as "incredible," wrote to Hogg. (p. 162)
[The letter obviously belongs to 1815.]

20. Shelley's notion of bringing in the millennium was by an
apocalyptic lightning bolt (until, *in the last few months of his*

life, he came to perceive that "the march of the human mind is slow"), whereas Darwin thought in terms of ages. (p. 270) [Shelley learned this lesson thoroughly during his Irish campaign of 1812.]

In conclusion, I must say that it has been a very disagreeable task to write this article. If, however, it is helpful in relegating *The Shelley Legend* to its rightful place as a semi-popular and thoroughly unreliable book, I shall have no further regrets. For the knowing reader the following statement by Professor Smith would have been a sufficient commentary on his ability to make sound judgments on Shelley affairs: "For the beginner, perhaps the best brief one volume account of Shelley that can be had is, even today, [R. H.] Stoddard's *Anecdote Biography of Shelley* [1876]" (p. 195; repeated on p. 260). Unfortunately, few knowing readers have been reviewers of *The Shelley Legend*.

𝔄 𝔑𝔢𝔴 𝔖𝔥𝔢𝔩𝔩𝔢𝔶 𝔏𝔢𝔤𝔢𝔫𝔡[1]

KENNETH N. CAMERON

THE FACT that Shelley's life contained so much of the romantic and the dramatic is unfortunate. Almost all the full length studies of him—Dowden's, Ingpen's, Peck's, White's—have been biographical rather than critical. And this has inevitably led to a falsity of evelution and perspective. We tend so easily to get lost in interminable controversies on the events of his life and forget that the essential value of biographical studies is the guidance they give to the under-standing of the works. If Shelley had not written *Prometheus Unbound* and *The Cenci*, the *Philosophical View of Reform* or the *Defence of Poetry* or *Adonais*, none would care whether he had treated Harriet well or ill, whether he was happy or unhappy with Mary, whether or not he had sexual relations with Claire. These events would long ago have been buried, along with similar events in the lives of millions of others, in obscurity. This shifting of evaluation and loss of perspective is even more acutely felt when a critic singles out such events and treats them in isolation as representative of the man as a whole. This is the case with the latest study. In *The Shelley Legend*, Professor Smith and his colleagues believe that they are presenting a new picture of Shelley, whereas they are only examining certain aspects of his sex life.

[1] Originally published in *The Journal of English and Germanic Philology* (XLV, October, 1946, 369-379), and reprinted here by permission of the author and of the Editor.

The Shelley Legend falls into three main parts: a bibliographical examination of some letters on Harriet; a biographical study of Shelley's relations with Harriet, Mary, Claire, etc.; and an attempted exposé of the development—from Mary Shelley to Newman I. White—of what the authors believe to be a false picture of Shelley. In all three parts, in addition to the basic lack of perspective just mentioned, the work is marred by serious internal defects. It is sensational rather than scholarly in its approach; there is little objective weighing of evidence; contradictory and incompatible arguments are allowed to exist almost side by side; the method of presentation is frequently tortuous and confused (different sections of the same topic being sometimes discussed fifty or a hundred pages apart); the research is at times astonishingly superficial, errors of fact being perpetrated that a few minutes' consultation in Dowden or White would have cleared up. Nevertheless, *The Shelley Legend* is not an entirely untrue book. In spite of its faults, the observations of its author are— especially in dealing with the ethical views of the early Shelley circle—frequently acute. The danger, however, is not so much that these segments of truth may be lost as that the whole portrait be accepted—as, indeed, it has been by many popular reviewers.

The first important bibliographical investigation in the book is that of the famed December 16, 1816 letter which Shelley sent to Mary at Bath on Harriet descending "the steps of prostitution." This letter has been known for some time to exist in several forged copies; one copy, owned by Thomas J. Wise, had, however, been thought by some authorities (notably De Ricci) to be genuine. This Wise copy has one peculiarity which had, on the other hand, caused other authorities (notably Blunden and Pollard) to be skeptical of it: the letter bears two postmarks, one for 1816 and one (incredibly) for 1859; and after the 1859 mark is written "not to be found." For this copy, Smith adds to the evidence of Blunden and Pollard the service of a handwriting expert and attempts to establish a provenance. The work of the handwriting expert seems plausible; but the attempted provenance is weak. Smith contends, in brief, that the letter was forged in 1848 by Major Byron; purchased by the Shelley family in 1851; mailed out by the Shelley family or some person unknown in 1859; acquired, subsequent to 1867, by John Tilley, a post office official who handed it over to Spencer Shelley; sold by Mrs. Spencer Shelley to H. Buxton Forman in 1908 and later given by Forman to Wise.[2] The weak link in this provenance is clearly the remailing of the letter in 1859; for it seems fantastic that anyone should in 1859 mail out a letter addressed to Mary Shelley at Bath in 1816 and already stamped as having gone through the post office in that year.

A satisfactory explanation for this strange business was advanced by Graham Pollard in the London *Times* in 1937.[3] Pollard refers to the discovery by Edmund Blunden that in 1859 a Mr. C. H. Taylor wrote to Leigh Hunt with the extraordinary information that he had just found a letter from Shelley to Mary on Harriet which had lain in the post office ever since 1816. This story was clearly a fake because the Shelley family had a copy of the letter at least as early as 1851; and the obvious explanation was that Taylor was either a forger or a forger's agent (not, as De Ricci thought, a "wide awake collector" who rummaged through dead letter offices). And the 1859 stamp on the letter identified it with that later owned by Wise. Pollard then pointed out that the written notation on the letter following the 1859 mark "not to be found," must be a forgery because post office regulations in 1859 demanded a special stamp on all undeliverable letters

---

[2] *The Shelley Legend*, pp. 84-98.
[3] *London Times Literary Supplement*, 1937, pp. 292, 364.

and not a mere notation; hence the 1859 postmark was forged and the letter was never mailed out in 1859 at all.[4] And if that postmark was forged probably the 1816 mark was forged also and hence the whole letter almost certainly a forgery.

So what we are dealing with is, most probably, two letters and not, as Smith believes (p. 97), one: number one purchased by the Shelley family in 1851; number two forged in 1859. What happened to the one purchased by the Shelley family we do not know. The 1859 forgery—after Hunt refused to bite—was acquired by Tilley and passed on successively to Spencer Shelley, Forman, and Wise. Only one piece of evidence connects the two letters, a statement by Wise in 1927 that his copy had once been owned by Sir Percy Florence and Lady Shelley. This statement, however, is contradicted by the fact that when in 1867 Spencer Shelley sent a copy of the letter to Lady Shelley for examination, she not only failed to claim it as her long lost letter mysteriously mailed in 1859, but declared it to be a forgery (p. 92). In the face of the evidence, and as Wise lies in the same statement in declaring (p. 87) he had had the letter for 28 years (whereas Forman only bought it in 1908), I think his whole statement can safely be discarded.

Professor Smith and his colleagues next examine copies of two other letters attacking Harriet (January 11, 1817 to Mary and January 17, 1817 to Byron) and declare them also to be forgeries (along with a letter of November 4, 1814 to Mary). This declaration is not backed up by an examination of either originals or even (as with the December 16 letter) photostats, and is based mainly on alleged peculiarities of

---

[4] Smith uses as his main argument (e.g., p. 89) that the letter was actually mailed in 1859 and on this he bases his provenance; but in other places (pp. 90, 103) he admits the possibility of Pollard's argument that it was not mailed and that the 1859 postmark was a forgery, without apparently seeing that if this be true his provenance collapses.

provenance. Having thus cleared the ground by declaring every letter that berates Harriet a forgery, Professor Smith draws conclusions:

> . . . we conclude that the commonly accepted story of Harriet Westbrook's dereliction, suicide and death is based upon forged and fallacious materials, and that she died wholly innocent of the charges of infidelity and prostitution levied against her in these forged documents. (p. 132)

The object of the forger was "to convict Harriet of prostitution and thus relieve Shelley of all blame" (p. 102). Knowing that these letters were forged, Mary Shelley, first, and then Lady Shelley, purchased them with the intention of besmirching Harriet and whitewashing Shelley. Smith hints that Mary was in league with the forger: "We shall not go further than De Ricci, for want of evidence, in speculating how much he did her bidding or catered to her whims and suggestions. . . . Were these forged letters, which contain such derogatory statements about Harriet and praises of Mary, wholly the product of Major Byron's invention . . . ?" (p. 122). These forged letters have, subsequently, been used by such biographers of Shelley as Dowden, Peck, and White "with the resultant drastic warping of both his biography and the interpretation of his character" (pp. 132-133).

Now, it is clear that in these conclusions Professor Smith has gone well beyond anything he has so far proven; for he here assumes that not only are the copies of the letters he has discussed forgeries but that there never existed genuine originals. True, he wavers on this issue, in some places assuming no originals (his central argument) and in others (pp. 110, 124, 304) hinting that originals may have existed, without appearing to realize that most of his case is destroyed if such originals did exist.

The evidence, indeed, points very strongly to the existence

of such originals, though whether they are at present extant we do not know. Following the controversy in the London *Times* in 1937 by Pollard and others on the December 16 letter, White pointed out (*Shelley* I, 723) that, regardless of whether the Wise version was a forgery, there must have existed a genuine original from which the forgery was made because Mary answered the letter on December 17 from Bath; and the original manuscript of Mary's letter is extant (in the Bodleian). An examination of Mary's letter shows that it answers Shelley's on at least six points; it is, therefore, undoubtedly an answer to the December 16 letter. The only way that Smith can extricate himself from the difficulty in which this places him is to show that Mary's letter is also a forgery; but for this, although he breathes sinister allegations (p. 112), he can produce no evidence; and—according to a conversation I once had with a person who had examined the manuscript of this letter—there is no indication of a forgery. One would think that a serious scholar would at least have secured a photostat of Mary's letter from the Bodleian before continuing his investigations on a point so crucial to his argument.

A second indication that originals lie behind these letters is the marked difference between them and the other Major Byron forgeries as published by Moxon. These Moxon letters are obvious forgeries, patched together from bits of previously published material in periodicals, Mary's editions of Shelley's prose and so on. But these letters on Harriet have no such possible sources. They could only be the products of one unusually familiar with Shelley's life in the winter of 1816-17 and talented enough to imitate his style. There is no evidence that Major Byron had either of these qualifications, and, indeed, every indication that he did not.

Major Byron must, therefore, have obtained possession of some original letters. How did he get them? The most probable answer is, from a desk which Mary left at Marlow in February 1818 when departing for Italy. This desk, containing the Harriet letters, was left in the charge of their friend Madocks. Professor Smith claims that Mary got the desk back in 1823, citing as his evidence "the letters of Shelley and Mary," (without giving a single specific reference), and Lady Shelley's statement that "on Shelley's death Mrs. Shelley sent for her desk and received it" (p. 92). On the basis of this evidence Professor Smith concludes that no forgeries were made from the letters in the desk because there was "no reason why anyone should have forged copies of the letters in Mary's Marlow desk between 1817 and 1823 when such letters had no market value for anyone" (p. 93). But "the letters of Shelley and Mary" do not state anywhere that I can find that Mary received the letters; and two items indicate that Lady Shelley was mistaken in assuming that she had. In April, 1823, almost a year after Shelley's death, Peacock, in reply to Mary's urgent requests for the letters left at Marlow, informed her that he was sending everything "with the exception of the Marlow papers, which I cannot procure without a second visit for that purpose." In 1845 when Mary was approached by Major Byron (*via* Hookham) her letters indicate that she has no doubt that he has got hold of some original letters which had been stolen from her: "As those he showed you are only a small portion of those lost, has he any more?"; "The letters were stolen—they were entrusted to a [word illegible] we thought honest and stolen."[5] This latter seems a pretty clear reference to Madocks (who we know had some Shelley manuscripts as late as 1857). There is indication, also, that Major Byron somehow got hold of the letters in the stolen desk. When Moxon saw William White in 1848, he informed him that "private letters," left by Mary

[5] *The Letters of Mary W. Shelley,* ed. by Frederick L. Jones (University of Oklahoma Press, 1944), II, 266, 268.

at Marlow, "had fallen in the hands of Mr. Byron."[6] And
when White himself later saw Byron, Byron informed him
that he had obtained some letters "he thought from the
Marlow box."[7] Hence, the evidence indicates that Mary did
not get the letters back either in 1823 or later; there is no
reason to assume the letters were forged "between 1817 and
1823," and every reason to assume that they were forged later
(1845-48) when they did have commercial value. Further,
the evidence indicates that Major Byron did have some
originals. It is, of course, possible that he could have forged
copies from these so accurate that Mary could not have detected them (for it would have been more profitable for him
to forge several copies and sell them as originals than to sell
one original only); but Mary would not have been fooled
by letters addressed to herself—as the two key letters under
discussion were—letters on so vital a subject as Harriet's suicide, *which had no originals.* There can be no doubt, from the
tenor of Mary's letters, that she believed she was getting
genuine Shelley letters, the contents of many of which were
engraved in her memory. Professor Smith attempts to extricate himself from this dilemma by his hints that Mary was in
league with the forger. But there is no evidence to support
such a charge; and the fact that Mary and Major Byron were,
at one point, at such loggerheads that court action was threatened over possession of the letters[8]—not to mention her general abuse of Byron and his "species of rascality," in her letters
to Hookham—make such a conclusion extremely untenable.

A few other items of evidence indicate not only originals for
the letters, but a base for the charges in them beyond the letters themselves. As Professor Smith records, Godwin made a

[6] William White, *The Calumnies of the Athenaeum Journal Exposed*
(London, 1852), p. 9.
[7] *Ibid.*, p. 12.
[8] Jones, *ed. cit.*, II, 264 n.

statement in a letter to William Baxter of May 12, 1817 that
Harriet "latterly lived in open connection with a colonel
Maxwell" (p. 116). In 1825, Keats' friend Charles Brown
made similar statements, giving as his source "Leigh Hunt
and another friend of Shelley's" (p. 27). If, then, both Hunt[9]
and Godwin had heard the charges against Harriet, there is
nothing extraordinary in their appearing in a private letter
of Shelley's (however much we may regret that Shelley ever
made such accusations). Furthermore, there exists a certain
basis for the charges in the statement of Harriet's landlady
at the inquest that she had been pregnant and the report in
the *Times* when her body was taken from the river that she
was "far advanced in pregnancy." In one place (p. 114) Smith
seems to accept Crabb Robinson's doubts as to whether Harriet
was pregnant, at another he suggests that Shelley was the
father (p. 206). But this latter charge is sheer gossip; and
what evidence we do possess is in the opposite direction. The
last recorded meeting between Harriet and Shelley was in
April, 1815; in March, 1816, relations between the two were
so strained that Harriet had to be forced by court order
to allow their son Charles to be presented by Shelley in a
Chancery case; nor does Smith mention that as Shelley was
out of England from May to September he could not possibly
have been the father if "well advanced" meant anything
between three and seven months (Harriet dying in November).

Professor Smith next presents Browning's story to Swinburne and Rossetti (apparently based on letters from Harriet)
that Shelley in 1814 left Harriet with but "14 shillings altogether." On this Professor Smith comments: "As Oedipus
exclaimed: 'All comes clear at last.' There is little room for
further doubt that we have here the true story of Harriet . . .

---

[9] Thornton Hunt, as Smith does not mention, also heard a similar story:
"Shelley, by One Who Knew Him," *Atlantic Monthly*, XI, 197 (1863).

the same story which Sir Percy and Lady Shelley stopped by seizing Hogg's Mss." (p. 205). But this story, whether circulated by Harriet or not, cannot be true, because on or about July 14, 1814 (i.e., the day of the first interview with Harriet to tell her of his love for Mary), Shelley wrote to Harriet: "If you want to draw on the Bankers before I see you, Hookham will give you the checks." And as we know that Shelley on July 6 deposited £1,100 in the bank there was presumably a fair amount there (even though some of it went to Godwin). It seems, further, fairly certain that Harriet received some of this account, as Shelley in his letter to her from Troyes on August 13, warned her: "Do not part with any of your money." And this could hardly refer to 14 shillings. In the same letter Shelley informed her that he had drawn up deeds and a settlement for a separate maintenance for her with a lawyer before leaving London. When, in the following June, Sir Bysshe's estate was finally settled and Shelley received an annual income of £1,000, he immediately settled £200 of this on Harriet. Later, in the fall of 1816, when he made his first will, he bequeathed £6,000 to Harriet and £10,000 to her children. That Shelley's desertion of Harriet was brutal and selfish no objective critic would deny but there is no point in dragging up ancient slanders as revelation which a few minutes' consultation in Dowden or White would suffice to refute. What Smith seems to forget, not only here but elsewhere, is that we are dealing with a family in-law quarrel and it is just as inadvisable to accept—as he does with a strange naïveté for so usually incredulous a critic—the stories of the Westbooks, as to accept those of Lady Shelley.

Professor Smith's investigation of these letters on Harriet, in spite of the fact that he does bring up new pieces of information, is essentially unsatisfactory. His provenance for the December 16 letter is decidedly shaky; his assumption of no originals for the letters, contradictory to the weight of the evidence; his belief that the charges against Harriet depend only on those letters is untrue; his charges against Mary Shelley are unfounded and those against Lady Shelley exaggerated; and his view that the acceptance of these letters by the biographers has resulted in any "drastic warping" of Shelley's character is, in consequence, without foundation.

In addition to the examination of these letters, the only other bibliographical discussion of consequence is that on the facsimile of the manuscript of *A Proposal for Putting Reform to the Vote* published by the Shelley Society. This facsimile Professor Smith claims, on the basis of handwriting, to be a forgery, but although the handwriting does not seem to be Shelley's there is no discernible reason why anyone would make so meticulous a forgery—even to the copying of blottings, erasures and interlineations—of a minor political tract.

Following his treatment of the Harriet episode Professor Smith goes on to examine other aspects of Shelley's sex life. His purpose here is to depict Shelley as a Don Juan, and his method is to suggest that Shelley had sexual relations with every woman he ever knew—Elizabeth Hitchener, Cornelia Turner, Fanny Imlay, Claire Clairmont, Sophia Stacey, Emilia Viviani, Jane Williams. On only three of these, Fanny Godwin, Claire Clairmont, Jane Williams, does he attempt to present any evidence, and on only one, Claire, is the evidence of any consequence.

His treatment of the suicide of Fanny Imlay is distinctly unhappy. After giving the statement of the notoriously gossipy Mrs. Godwin that Fanny was in love with Shelley and quoting Shelley's verse ("Friend had I known thy secret grief,") on her, he continues:

Moreover, there are evidences that Shelley, then living in Marlow, was with her in London on September 11th and again on the 24th. No explanation of Shelley's having gone to Bristol on September 30, ten days before Fanny's suicide, as recorded in the journal for that date, has been forthcoming. Biographers have either overlooked or have attempted no explanation of what Shelley was doing in Bristol on that date. . . . So far as is known Shelley was the only man to enter her life, and the only man closely associated with her in these days immediately before her death on October 9, 1816. (p. 218)

These comments build up a case on innuendo and half truth which it is difficult to justify. Smith gives the impression of three assignations between Shelley and Fanny in the weeks preceding her death, on September 11, September 24, and September 30. He does not state the source for these items of information, thus leaving the impression of hidden mysteries. The first date, however (which should be September 10 and not 11), is to be found in a letter from Shelley to Byron on September 11, in which Shelley—living in London, not, as Smith implies, in Marlow—tells Byron that Fanny has seen him the day before in connection with a loan for Godwin.

By September 14, Shelley was in Marlow; on September 19—as Professor Smith neglects to mention—Mary joined him there; both stayed in Marlow until September 24, on which day Shelley went to London to negotiate some more business for Godwin and there met Fanny, apparently in a business office in Piccadilly (as Fanny herself informed Mary in a letter of October 3). In neither of these meetings is there the slightest hint of anything beyond business transactions. Fanny's letters, in fact, reveal a most unromantic single-track obsession with raising money for Godwin.

As for the third date (September 30), Smith here hints that Shelley made a secret visit to Fanny in Bristol (tactfully ignored by the biographers). This, however, was impossible as Fanny did not leave London for Bristol until October 7.[10]

[10] Kegan Paul, *William Godwin, His Friends and Contemporaries* (London, 1876), II, 241 f. Paul quotes a local newspaper of Saturday, October 12, in which it was stated that Fanny "told a fellow-passenger that she came

Nor does Smith inform his readers that Shelley had been absent from England from May to September, so that no prolonged affair can have taken place in the months preceding the suicide, and he leaves out the considerable evidence that Fanny had been almost frantically despondent for many months as a result of her sad situation in the Godwin household. This, of course, does not mean that Fanny, an introverted, unattractive girl, did not nurse a secret longing for Shelley and that this did not play some part in her general despair; but there is certainly no evidence that Shelley in the months before her death in any way encouraged this feeling.

Professor Smith's treatment of the Jane Williams episode is even less substantial. (Rossetti once remarked of Hogg's *Life of Shelley* that he hated a man who wrote "by nudges and winks." He should have lived to read *The Shelley Legend.*) Peck once tried to build up a similar case by reference to a letter from Shelley to Byron which apparently told all. Unfortunately, Peck was unable either to produce the letter or say where it could be found. The only new item added by Professor Smith is his peculiar interpretation of the story of Jane and Shelley in the boat: "his passion culminated in the suggestion that they overturn the boat and die together" (p. 11). But there is no hint of any such suicide-pact "passion" in the story, as Trelawny, our only source, gives it as an example of Shelley's rather whimsical melancholy. Nor does Smith mention that Jane's children were with her in the boat. Nor, finally, does he—although he is usually fond of quoting Trelawny's comments to Rossetti—give his flat statement as taken down by Rossetti: "He is certain there was no intrigue

---

to Bath by the mail from London on Tuesday morning [Oct. 8], from whence she proceeded to Bristol." Paul also states definitely that she left London on October 7, and as he had been relying for most of such information on Godwin's diary, I presume he found this fact also recorded there.

between Shelley and Mrs. Williams."[11] And as Trelawny was living with or near Shelley during much of the time of his acquaintance with the Williamses he had opportunity to know.

As to most of the rest of "the roll call of Shelley's women friends," the sharers with him of the delights of "the vagaries of free love coteries," Smith contents himself with ogling hints. Whether or not Shelley had relations with any of them is unknown, but that he had with most of them is unlikely. It is difficult, for instance, to imagine him as a buoyant youth of 19 making very ardent love to a rangy schoolmistress of 29, or as a man of 27 being passionately stirred by the crinoline gigglings of Miss Sophia Stacey (who, by the way, was most formidably chaperoned). Nor would one imagine a convent the most convenient of assignation places (in addition to which Trelawny informed Rossetti that he was sure that Shelley and Emilia were communing purely on a Platonic level).[12] That Shelley was attracted to Cornelia Turner is true, but his letter to Hogg on October 3, 1814 gives no hint that the affair progressed beyond an inactive worship stage.

The case for Shelley as Don Juan, therefore, is distinctly weak. On the other hand, there is evidence to indicate a love affair between Shelley and Claire Clairmont, and one between Mary and Hogg. To neither of these possible affairs, however, do Professor Smith and his colleagues add much that we did not already know. The Shelley-Claire affair was first suggested, at least in any substantial form, by John Harrington Smith in 1939.[13] He believed that the affair took place in the spring of 1815 and was of brief duration, and that Claire was not the mother of the Neapolitan child. His arguments were answered, not, it seems to me, too convincingly,

[11] William Michael Rossetti, *Rossetti Papers, 1862-1870* (London, 1903), p. 502.
[12] *Ibid.*
[13] "Shelley and Claire Clairmont," *PMLA*, LIV, 785-814 (1939).

by Professors White and Jones.[14] The possible affair between Hogg and Mary was first revealed by White in his *Shelley* (1940) although he was not permitted to publish the actual letters involved (nor was Jones in his edition of Mary's letters in 1944). The letters were first published by Walter Sidney Scott in *Harriet and Mary* (The Golden Cockerel Press, England, 1944). The events revealed in these letters and in the journals of Shelley and Mary can be interpreted in two ways. White and Scott feel that they indicate nothing beyond a friendship between Shelley and Claire to which Mary responded by threats of an affair with Hogg; Jones believes that Mary was "trying to force herself to love Hogg," but that there is no evidence that they had relations.[15] On the other hand, Smith and his colleagues take the view that Claire and Shelley were having an affair in 1815, that Hogg and Mary were also then having an affair, and that Claire was the mother and Shelley the father of the Neapolitan child.

In regard to the events of 1815, the journals and letters certainly indicate that love affairs were planned. Such is the patent meaning of Mary's and Shelley's letters to Hogg, and if the Mary-Hogg affair took place, then the hints and deletions in the journals point strongly towards a parallel Shelley-Claire affair. Both affairs, however, if they materialized must have been of comparatively short duration. Mary was pregnant until February 22, her baby died on March 6; she can therefore have been prepared neither physiologically nor psychologically to receive Hogg's ardors until the middle of March at least; and by late April her letters show that the cautious Hogg is shying away. ("Do you mean to come down

---

[14] Newman I. White, *Shelley* (New York, 1940), 1, 694; Frederick L. Jones, "Mary Shelley and Claire Clairmont," *South Atlantic Quarterly*, XLII, 409-412 (1943). Smith answered White in "Shelley and Claire Again," *Studies in Philology*, XLI, 94-105 (1944).

[15] Jones, *ed. cit.*, 1, 7 n.

to us? I suppose not, Prince Prudent.") By May, Claire had left the household and was living in Devon (although Shelley perhaps visited her there in July). Where Smith gets the January 1818 date for the final letter in the series—thus giving the impression of an affair extending over three years —he does not state. Scott, who examined the original manuscript, dated it April 27, 1815.[16]

If these affairs did take place there seems to be cause neither for horror—for extra-marital relations are scarcely an unknown phenomenon—nor surprise—for they would be in accord with Shelley's views. Shelley's sex ethic will be found, most succinctly, in his review of Hogg's *Alexy Haimatoff* and his *Discourse on the Manners of the Ancients Relative to the Subject of Love*. In brief it was that although sensuality without love as a basis for sexual relations was abhorrent, people genuinely in love should have relations regardless of marriage ties; sexual relations must be viewed only as one segment of a complex emotional relationship. If, therefore, Shelley and Claire felt themselves to be in love they would have had relations (and it does not seem to be of much consequence whether they did or not); and similarly Shelley would feel that he could not stand in Mary's way if she wished the same privileges he took himself.

In regard to the Neapolitan child, Smith adds no new evidence. He examines the materials as presented by Professor White and comes to opposite conclusions. He makes a good case to show that the child was not adopted (and White's argument here has never appeared very convincing), but a weaker case to show that it was Shelley's and Claire's. If the child was Shelley's and Claire's why were the Gisbornes informed of its existence? Surely, so dread a secret would be kept tightly hidden. Or why did the Shelleys feel sure enough of their ground to enter into legal negotiations to sue Foggi

[16] Scott, *ed. cit.*, p. 45.

for slander? Can we dismiss as a tissue of lies Shelley's letter to Mary and Mary's answer to Mrs. Hoppner with its flat statement—"Claire had no child"? Nor do Claire's horse-back-riding and mountain ascending activities seem indicative of pregnancy. Professor Smith makes little attempt at a serious evaluation of the mass of conflicting and often confusing evidence but gives rather the impression of a somewhat frenetic desire to prove a case. The Neapolitan child must still be chalked up as a mystery, and the whole controversy has, it seems to me, been exaggerated out of proportion to its importance.

Taking Shelley's sex life as a whole, we can conclude that while it was unusual in certain aspects—his attitude towards the projected Hogg-Mary affair, for instance—, it is far from unique: he left a wife with whom he was unhappy for another woman, whom he later married; he perhaps also had extra-marital relations during one or two periods of his life with one other woman. If he had other affairs also we have no knowledge of them, but what evidence we possess makes it unlikely. Such a sexual history placed in comparison with one by an average young male from one of our present day "advanced" sets would pale into insignificance. Certainly it does not justify Professor Smith's "kiss and garters" (p. 162) air of sybaritic revelation.

The third section of Professor Smith's book—I call it a third section although materials for it are scattered throughout and often take a good deal of putting together—deals with the development of Shelley biography. His picture of this development runs somewhat as follows: Lady Shelley, terrified lest the facts of Shelley's sex life should become public, made herself the center of a conspiracy to keep these facts hidden; in this conspiracy she influenced the nineteenth century Shelley scholars, especially Garnett and Dowden (with Garnett playing a kind of "second murderer" role), to accept the picture of Shelley as a "Victorian angel"; she used forged letters and bowdlerized the Shelley and Mary journals; she was instrumental in organizing the Shelley Society and seems somehow to be directing its activities behind the scenes; her "Victorian angel" concept of Shelley later penetrated the Shelley biographical tradition and is to be found even in White. As a result of these sinister proclivities Shelley's biography is on an unsound basis (p. 258) and "Shelley scholarship . . . kept at least three or four removes from truth" (p. 212).

That there is some truth to Smith's charges there can be no doubt, but they are exaggerated to an absurd point. Lady Shelley certainly did everything possible to hush up the facts on the desertion of Harriet, but that she had any inkling of the other exhibits in Smith and company's Chamber of Horrors is most unlikely. Nor did her "conspiracy" take on the spiderlike universality that is here attributed to it. That she had much to do with the Shelley Society[17] is unlikely, and what Smith means by her influence on biography is the failure of biographers to depict Shelley as Don Juan. Now that there has been a good deal of romantic idealization in dealing with Shelley's sex life is true, and this is exhibited most conspicuously in Glynn Gryll's biographies of Mary and Claire, but Smith's concept is as much an extreme in one direction as Lady Shelley's is in the other. Smith's general implication that modern Shelley biography, especially White's, is unreliable, arises from his obsession that forgeries form the foundation of that biography. The vast mass of the material for Shelley biography, however, has been well sifted and neither forged versions of four letters that are clearly based on originals nor Lady Shelley's changes in the journals—which do

---

[17] Smith gives no evidence for this but cites Julia Power's *Shelley in America in the Nineteenth Century* as his source; Miss Power, however, also fails to give either evidence or reference.

not appear to be major—disturb this main base. This, of course, by no means precludes new discoveries or new interpretations.

One of the weakest aspects of Professor Smith's book is his concept of Shelley as a poet. He compares Shelley to Swinburne (p. 211) as "pouring forth meaningless onomatopoeia," —a notion as quaintly Victorian as any he attacks—, and he accepts as gospel Santayana's angelic school simperings on Shelley as "a bee or a butterfly" (p. 307 f.). *The Cenci* becomes—shades of Mrs. Grundy!—"that doubtful drama" (p. 267); and its worth as a stage play is judged on the basis of the shocked utterance of the more conservative Victorian critics. (Professor Smith does not seem to have heard of a later stage history.) From this simple failure to know what Shelley's philosophy or poetry is about flows that tone of satiric ridicule which underlies the whole book. Smith essentially views Shelley—in spite of occasional beadsman mumblings about his "greatness"—as nothing but a crackpot freelover whose family are trying to cover up his escapades. Hence the only reason to establish Shelley Societies, to set up monuments, or to write biographies is to prove the respectability of the prodigal. That a group of serious scholars could establish a Shelley Society or do research for no other reason than to study the works of a great poet, does not occur to Smith. On the other hand, all who have cast ridicule on Shelley—from Hogg[18] to Aldous Huxley—are clearly men of perspicacity who have seen through the family plot. Thus, Shelley scholarship is metamorphosed into a kind of divorce court comedy.

Although on the whole the work is not badly documented, some carelessness is apparent. "George Barnefield" is declared, without reference, to be Edward Carpenter (p. 301),

[18] Professor Smith's almost devotional trust in Hogg (e.g., pp. 174-177) seems at variance with his usual abhorrence of fabricators.

one Edith Wyatt, is quoted, apparently as a Shelley authority, but even the name of the work containing the quotation is not given (p. 157). Jones' references to Mary's desk in his edition of her letters are indicated simply by *passim*, which is of no help, as the desk is not mentioned in the index, and one is presumably supposed to plow through two large volumes looking for references to desks. A most learned disquisition (pp. 58–61) is given on the sources of the forged Moxon letters which one might presume to be by Smith and his colleagues if it were not for a reference in De Ricci to a "remarkable collection of letters and cuttings relating to these forgeries," made by Sir Frederick Madden and now residing in the New York Public Library.[19]

In spite of its errors and distortions, what does *The Shelley Legend* add to the sum total of Shelley scholarship? I would list its main contributions as follows (although qualifications are necessary in some items): a fuller exposé than heretofore of Major Byron and his activities relating to Shelley; a further demonstration that the Wise version of the December 16, 1817 letter is a forgery; additional but not always trustworthy material on the provenances of four letters; an exposé of the further chicaneries of Wise (in the Shelley Society); a frequently sharp but unbalanced analysis of the existing material on the Neapolitan child mystery which implies the need for further research and re-examination of the evidence; an introduction of the diaries of Crabb Robinson and William Michael Rossetti as more important items for Shelley biography than had been previously thought. This material properly integrated into a balanced biography will be useful. In spite of these and a few other nuggets of truth in a ton or so of very mixed ore, however, Professor Smith and his colleagues essentially accomplish little more than the setting up

[19] Seymour De Ricci, *A Bibliography of Shelley's Letters* (Privately Printed, 1927), p. 294.

of a new Shelley legend. Their basic concept of Shelley—a "romantic, pagan Shelley"—is as false as the "Vicorian angel" concept they so manfully set out to destroy. Shelley was essentially neither the one nor the other, but a great revolutionary poet and thinker, a scholar of wide culture and deep philosophical and political understanding, a writer of a versatility almost unmatched in the history of English literature, a man of broad, humanitarian understanding. Of this Shelley, the essential Shelley, we find nothing in *The Shelley Legend.*

14

17

19

21

25

38

88

90

95

102

106

108